# The New Crusaders

## The Corporate Social Responsibility Debate

Douglas J. Den Uyl

TER

ISBN 0-912051-03-5

## TABLE OF CONTENTS

## ACKNOWLEDGEMENTS

I wish to take this opportunity to thank a number of the people who made this monograph possible. First of all I wish to thank Liberty Fund, Inc. for backing a conference on Business Ethics in 1981. This conference, attended by businessmen, philosophers, and economists, inspired this monograph. I would therefore like to thank all the participants of that conference, especially the following businessmen: Joseph Mullen, Robert S. Brown, Herbert Corneulle, and William Burleigh. I would also like to thank Jennifer Roback of the economics department at Yale for sending me some helpful information. In addition, the Social Philosophy and Policy Center at Bowling Green State University has been most helpful—in particular, Ellen Paul. Special thanks are owed to Fred D. Miller, Jr. of Bowling Green State University for his comments and patience with earlier drafts of this monograph. Finally, my wife, Janet Mullen Den Uyl, has made it possible for me to live vicariously through her in the contemporary American business world. For over a decade we have seen the best and worst American business has to offer, and it is to her business acumen and personal integrity that I dedicate what follows.

When Pyrrhus had thus retired into Epirus, and left Macedonia, he had a fair occasion given him by fortune to enjoy himself in quiet, and to govern his own kingdom in peace. But he was persuaded, that neither to annoy others, nor to be annoyed by them, was a life insufferably languishing and tedious. (Plutarch)

# I. Introduction

If the phrase, "the business of America is business," once characterized our national conscience, almost the opposite could be said today. Although business activities continue to expand, the media and public image of business is more negative than positive. Corporations are said to be exploiting their workers, polluting the environment, supporting racism and sexism, and even contributing to the ultimate destruction of mankind. The typical cartoon rendition of a businessman is that he is a cigar smoking fat man without any moral scruples. Such a person delights in taking advantage of the weak and innocent and corporate policies are directed towards such ends. Some have even said that to associate "business" and "ethics" in the same sentence is to contradict oneself. The pursuit of greed and power can never be ethical or moral. In similar fashion, some would argue that the pursuit of profits is necessarily anti-social, since profits encourage greed and greed is an anti-social passion.

The evidence for the stigma attached to business (especially large corporations) can be found not only in our daily papers and on television, but also in our academic institutions and churches. Within our colleges and universities a growing number of courses are being offered in "business ethics." In and of itself, there is nothing sinister in such offerings. Indeed, these courses can provide business students and others a way of studying the questions that arise in a pluralistic and technologically sophisticated social environment. However, if one reviews the textbooks and articles that characterize much of what is offered under the heading of "business ethics," either an anti-business bias is present or the market system is seen as an untamed beast in need of more government regulation to domesticate it. As of this writing, there are no textbooks in business ethics that even give advocates of the free market an *equal* voice with pro regulation or socialist authors.

The news is no better (indeed it is worse) if one turns one's attention to church groups. Many of these groups have adopted "corporate responsibility programs" which monitor corporate policies and protest those the groups believe to be morally wrong. The protests often take the form of proxy resolutions submitted to corporations and their stockholders. As we shall see, there is an ideological flavor to these proxy proposals. The thrust of most of the proposals is not to call for an end to obviously immoral behavior on the part of the corporations, but rather to push a questionable political program based upon an equally questionable ideology. Moreover, this trend is growing rather than diminishing. For example, an organization now exists called the "Interfaith Center on Corporate Responsibility" (ICCR). This organization seeks to focus the efforts of church groups (mostly Roman Catholic) protesting corporate policies. One of the vehicles of protest is the proxy resolution, and the ICCR has published a book containing those resolutions.[1] Here is how ICCR describes the level and direction of activities in the area of proxy resolutions:

> Church groups are submitting 118 resolutions to 85 companies as compared to 89 resolutions to 72 companies in 1982, 88 resolutions to 72 companies in 1981, 104 resolutions to 81 companies in 1980, 62 companies in 1979, and 47 in 1978. As summarized in the index, more than 100 church agencies are responsible for filing the various resolutions.[2]

The chapters which follow discuss both the academic theories and the particular proxy resolutions that are part of the debate over what is called "corporate social responsibility." A number of the proxy resolutions published by the ICCR are examined in detail as are some theories of corporate social responsibility found in current business ethics texts. My central purpose is to elucidate the biases and inadequacies inherent in both the theoretical and practical proposals of those demanding more "responsible" behavior on the part of corporations. Furthermore, I intend to show that the church groups examined here, and the theories that underlie their concerns, are by no means the only perspective available in this debate. This last point is especialy difficult to make, since most people associate moral values with their church. However, given the increased political activity of many church leaders and organizations, the simple equation of church and moral values can be questioned. Many of these groups advocate a particular *kind* of moral outlook—one that can be questioned even by members of the same faith.

The "corporate social responsibility" debate is primarily a moral issue. To many people a "moral issue" is one that concerns their personal morals, such as gambling, premarital sex, or drinking. But this is too limited a view of the matter. A moral issue is any issue that concerns what values one *ought* to have and thus what actions one *ought* to take in light of those values. Abortion, for example, is a moral issue because the central question is how one should value the fetus and thus how it should be treated. An example of a moral issue in business might be advertising. If we value truth, is an ad which does not tell the whole truth about the product immoral, and should people be allowed to produce such ads? Some moral issues are broader in scope than others. A question such as "is it right to lie about one's previous income when filling out a job application?" is much narrower than, "should corporations be allowed to pay more wages to some than others?" However broad or narrow the topic, moral issues concern the appropriateness of values and the actions that come from them.

The corporate social responsibility debate (henceforth to be designated as CSR) can be considered a moral issue because questions are raised about current practices, values, and policies that some claim ought to be changed. These demands for change do not often take the form that business practices, if changed, would be more efficient or produce more goods. Instead, the challenges are directed at the very values inherent in a market oriented system of production, and that makes these challenges moral challenges. Many of these challenges take what philosophers would call a "categorical" form. Businesses must stop (or be stopped) from doing one thing and do another instead. This claim is known as the "moral must." Businesses might be *able* to do otherwise, but they *must* not (are obligated not to) if their actions are to be morally proper. Thus what businesses are or are not obligated to do raises the theoretical question of *why* they ought to behave one way and not another. Chapters Two and Three which follow deal with the moral theory that stands behind arguments about the obligations of business. In Chapter Two I present and evaluate theories that interpret responsibility in terms of more interference with market processes. In Chapter Three, I offer my own views on the kind of moral principles that underlie and support a market order.

Chapters Four through Eight are concerned with more practical questions than are Chapters Two and Three. Using the principles described in Chapter Three, I analyze such topics as South Africa, plant closings, employment practices, pollution, and nuclear technology. One of the major purposes in these chapters is to show that those who claim to represent the *moral* side of the debate (as opposed to the practical or economic) have usurped that title. These groups do not represent morality *per se,* and their views are subject to question on moral grounds, let alone practical grounds. Thus, although a specific position is to be found in the pages that follow, my overall purpose is to maintain the integrity of the debate over CSR—a debate that has lapsed into little more than an ideological struggle.

The "ideological struggle" has now become so intense that many actually become impatient with the moral questions and theories that are part of the CSR controversy. Today moral debate often gives way to direct action or morally neutral analyses of how to meet responsibilities assumed to exist. The direct action approach was anticipated by Joel Henning ten years ago.[3] Henning argued that it is obvious that corporations are acting irresponsibly, and since it is almost equally obvious that corporations, by their very nature, cannot change to responsible behavior, what is needed is direct action toward further regulation and the restructuring of the corporate charter. This approach assumes that the fundamental moral questions have been solved. And today the concern of many is not *whether* to demand more "responsibility" from corporations, but *how* to do so. One approach is to "infiltrate the system" with lawyers, accountants, business school professors, and the like who know what must be done and will take steps to do it. There may still be some dispute about whether this or that proposal will "work" or bring about the desired changes. But many assume that moral theory has already condemned corporations, so that we no longer need to examine basic assumptions.

The position just described might be dismissed as simply the kind of conclusion one would expect from ideologues, radicals, or disgruntled activists. Nevertheless, there are similarities between the attitudes of some "Naderites" and more conventional analyses of CSR. By "conventional analyses" I mean discussions of CSR often found in "business and society" texts where the audience is primarily the business student rather than the humanities major. The trend in these texts is often one of assuming that there is no longer a question concerning the validity of the prevalent theories of CSR. The debate now seems to be one of deciding degrees and cases. Here is a representative sample:[4]

> It should also be stated that only a few business people or academics argue against the fundamental notion of social responsibility today. The debate among business people has more often centered on the kinds and degree of social responsibility, than on the basic question of whether business has it or not.

The implication, here, is that there is no longer any doubt about the correct moral posture. And like the social reformer mentioned above, this textbook attitude seeks to de-emphasize the basic moral component in favor of discussion of theories about how to insure responsible behavior.[5]

Perhaps, however, the most important example I can offer of recent attempts to remove the moral character of CSR is the call some have made to change the language from "corporate social responsibility" to "corporate social responsiveness."[6] The term "responsibility" has ethical connotations associated with it. "Responsiveness," on the other hand, seems to side-step ethics entirely by giving the impression that the issue here is only one of being responsive. This trend, too, is to be expected given the frequency with which the Davis/Blomstrom "Iron Law of Responsibility" has been cited in textbooks ("those who do not use power in a manner which society considers responsible will tend to lose it."). This "law," formulated over a decade ago, is thoroughly amoral; it does not recommend a course of action or describe appropriate values. Instead, it presents itself as a *description* of reality. It is interesting to note that in the revised version of the text from which this "law" first appeared, the authors use "responsiveness" rather than "responsibility" in their first chart.[7] All this clearly suggests a move away from ethical or moral (used interchangeably here) analysis. The impression one is left with is that only some philosophers and a few "traditionalists" ever question current notions of CSR.

CSR began as a moral position with social and political implications.The effort to change the focus of the debate from whether a certain approach to the question is justified to one of developing techniques for constructing laws or regulations may indeed succeed. But the question as to whether this "success" is itself responsible will remain. As we shall see, the basis upon which corporations are said to have special responsibilities is a tenuous and debatable one. In fact, much of the movement toward "responsiveness" may itself rest upon some rather questionable moral assumptions. The moral foundations cannot be escaped and are assumed even by those wishing to avoid such discussions. It is, therefore, necessary that we begin by discussing basic moral frameworks in order to arrive at a point where more particular questions can be answered.

# II. The Attack On Corporate Freedom and Responsibility

> The America people gotta stand up and be counted and forget this philosophical horses__t of free enterprise being a birthright.
>
> William Winpisinger, President, International Association of Machinists and Aerospace Workers.

On April 17, 1980 America witnessed its first "Big Business Day." The purpose of this event, which was well covered by the media, was summarized by William Wynn, President of the United Food and Commercial Workers Union: "Just as the 1950's scrutinized the labor movement and the 1970's big government, this Day will mark the 1980's as the decade to correct the abuses of big business."[1] The organizers of the event hoped that Big Business Day would help promote stricter federal controls over corporations. In fact, the event was carefully timed to coincide with the introduction of the Corporate Democracy Act in Congress. Mark Green, one of the organizers of Big Business Day, offered his assessment of the purpose and activities of Big Business Day:

> We intend to do for big business what Earth Day, Food Day and Sun Day did for their subjects—expose abuses and explore alternatives. In hundreds of communities across the nation there will be teach-ins and debates, alternatives-to-business fairs, the promotion of small business and appropriate technologies, "trials" of corrupt companies, nominations for a "Corporate Hall of Shame," symbolic "bread lines" at banks that red-line communities, and a compilation of models of corporate social responsibility.

Notice that both Green and Wynn speak of "abuses" and, thus, of the alleged *irresponsibility* of corporations. Green refers explicitly to the need for models of "corporate social responsibility."

What about this idea of "corporate social responsibility?" What does it mean, and what standards are used to decide whether a corporation is being responsible or not? Green himself suggests that we explore "models" of corporate social responsibility. This chapter and the next are devoted to just that. I shall examine three basic "models" that are used to ground claims about the responsibility (or lack thereof) of corporations. In this chapter I shall define the nature of these three models and take a critical look at two of them—the two that could be used by supporters of Big Business Day. One of these models, the Social Permission Theory, is most likely to underlie the thinking of corporate critics such as Green. Thus, I shall devote the bulk of my attention to that theory and argue that the principles espoused by the theory do not command our acceptance. In the next chapter, then, I shall discuss the theory that I believe to be most plausible. It should become clear after both chapters that basic theoretical assumptions can have and do have practical consequences.

## A. *Three Theories of Corporate Social Responsibility*

In a recent issue of the *Journal of Business Ethics,* Howard Sohn categorizes the main theories of CSR into four schools: the fundamentalist theory (more generally called the "traditionalist" or "classical" theory), the constituency theory, the legal framework theory, and the corporate citizenship theory.[2] The "fundamentalist" position is said to hold that corporations have no obligations beyond the pursuit of profits within a context of free and open competition. Sohn claims that Milton Friedman and Theodore Levitt are the most significant representatives of this theory.[3] Although Sohn gives each school its own unifying set of principles, it would be fair to say that the latter three schools take their bearings by opposing the fundamentalist theory. Sohn's last three theories could, therefore, be considered variations of a single category—the "social permission" theory.

The social permission theory holds that corporations exist and act by permission of society at large and/or the state.[4] Corporations are obligated to consider all possible "constituents" because all possible constituents make up society at large. These "constituents" were the ones who gave corporations permission to do business in the first place, and thus it is they to whom corporations are obligated (constituency theory). Moreover, if good behavior is not exhibited by corporations, those corporations can be considered "bad citizens" and be made to conform to a model of good citizenship (citizenship theory). Finally, the legal concept associated with the social permission theory has most commonly been known under the heading of the "concession theory"[5] or the "legal creator" theory.[6] This theory holds that corporations are creations of the state.

So far we have two theories of corporate social responsibility—the fundamentalist and social permission theories. The two main exponents of the fundamentalist theory—Levitt and Friedman—actually generate two *different* approaches to this issue—thus giving us three theories in total. One of these approaches could be called the "functional theory." This theory tends to conceive of the CSR debate in morally neutral or amoral terms. Corporations are believed to have certain functions or structural principles that dictate their role in society. For example, the idea that corporations have met their social responsibilities merely by obeying the law would fit here, since determining social welfare is the function of the state and not the corporation. People who talk in terms of corporate social responsiveness would fit under this theory as well. Their argument is that the very integrity and nature of a corporation is its responsiveness to changing circumstances and demand. Those that respond properly (to economic factors or otherwise) will survive, while those that do not respond properly will perish.[7] Thus, if the current climate of opinion demands that corporations be "socially responsible," then corporations must do so. Furthermore, arguments claiming that corporations must self-regulate to avoid an environment hostile to "free enterprise" would also come under the functionalist theory. These positions have in common their attempt to avoid appeals to moral principles in favor of appeals to the actual operating nature of business and society. The "father" of this position is Theodore Levitt,[8] although the functional view does not necessarily require agreement with Levitt's own conclusions.

Finally, there is the "individual agreement theory." Its most significant exponent is Milton Friedman.[9] It can fairly be said that this view is almost exactly the opposite of the social permission theory. For example, the "constituents" of business are *only* those who voluntarily enter into exchange agreements with the corporation. The responsibility to these constituents is to live up to the terms agreed upon. The responsibilities a corporation has to those who are not its constituents are simply to avoid violating their individual rights while the constituents are being served. This theory would also hold that corporations are not creatures of the state. The state simply recognizes the agreements reached by certain individuals or groups of individuals. This has been called the "legal recognition" theory, and it is opposed to the "legal creator" theory.[10] In sum, the only responsibilities recognized by this theory are for the corporation to engage "in open and free competition without deception or fraud."[11]

### B. *The Functional Theory*

If our goal is to determine whether and to what extent corporations have a responsibility to society, then one of these three theories should look the most attractive. Since I shall defend the individual agreement theory in the next chapter, it is important to examine the faults of the other two theories, here—especially since these theories are widely believed both inside and outside of the business community. Of the three schools just mentioned, the functional theory is the least attractive. It cannot be denied that this position has great short term pragmatic and rhetorical appeal. But in the final analysis, the functional view cannot offer any criteria for distinguishing the legitimate from the illegitimate claim or offer any form of consistent guidance. One way to demonstrate this last point is to examine in some detail Levitt's argument.

Levitt's argument depends upon some background assumptions that must be understood before his thesis can be evaluated. In the first place, Levitt assumes that monolithic power can be avoided only if society does not become dominated by the interests of any one group. The only way to insure that no group becomes dominant is to have an atmosphere of vigorous conflict among interest groups. Cooperation (e.g., between business and government) serves to entrench already established groups who then begin to monopolize power. Thus, each major interest group (business, labor, government, and agriculture) has a specific function to perform and should fight encroachments by other interest groups. Levitt, for example, sees the function of business to be profit maximization and the function of government to be concern for the general welfare. Given these preliminary remarks, Levitt's argument runs as follows:

1. Any business firm that engages in activities proper to labor, government, or agriculture is acting outside of its function.

2. Separate functions must be maintained if monolithic power is to be avoided.
3. Since we want to avoid monolithic power, no firm should act outside of its business function.
4. Welfare activities are the province of government.
5. Demands that corporations become "socially responsible" are demands that corporations engage in welfare functions.
6. Thus, business firms should not engage in welfare activities.

It is clear from this argument why Levitt has been classed with "conservatives" on the issue of CSR. Nevertheless, the argument could be used to justify the opposite conclusion!

First of all, Levitt implies that business and government should leave each other alone except when "vigorous conflict" is needed to thwart attempted encroachments. Suppose such a conflict takes place and the government wins the fight. Business could have no complaints after the battle was lost, because there are no standards to evaluate legitimate versus illegitimate encroachments, other than the process of interest group conflict itself. If the government is successful often enough, we could end up with the kind of state monitoring of business that we have today. Levitt cannot complain that profit maximization is illegitamately restricted with *every* government victory, for the very scope of the arena of profit maximization is itself determined by the *outcome* of preceding battles.[12] In addition, Levitt does not seem to object to government encroachment through taxation which certainly makes it impossible for government and business to remain completely separated.

More importantly, however, is Levitt's failure to realize that he assigns a more encompassing function to government than he does to business. If government is in charge of the general welfare, then business can only be one component in the welfare of all. Thus, if government decides that more regulation of business is in the general welfare, government would only be fulfilling its function by requiring business to obey. Indeed, if government decides that the general welfare calls for "socially responsible" attitudes and actions on the part of business, then business would have no legitimate claim to resist. Since many people today, as well as the government, are demanding more socially responsible actions of business, those who call for more social responsibility may be capturing more of the spirit of Levitt's argument than is Levitt himself.

To see how Levitt's argument can generate some conclusions contrary to the ones he intended, one need only slightly alter a few of Levitt's assumptions. For example, one could expand the list of major interest groups from four to six by simply including "consumers" and "environmentalists." "Business" would, now, be in combat with more than one or two groups, and the odds are that it would have to make concessions on profitability all the way around. One could also modify Levitt's statement about the function of a business from the narrow profit maximization principle to the broader function of using resources to "respond to people's needs." If the latter criterion were used, clearly Levitt's argument would generate more in the way of CSR than he allows.

Levitt's argument, and the possible variations of it, is fundamentally defective because of its amorality. Ultimately the argument suggests that the whole issue of CSR reduces to a power game—with business currently on the losing end of the struggle. The absurd length to which current recommendations for corporate submissiveness can go was demonstrated recently in a HARVARD BUSINESS REVIEW article that called for corporations to be "good puppies."[13] If morality and responsibility are equated with being "good puppies" in the corporate arena, it is no wonder that many who defend the role of the corporation are cynical about any attempt to bring moral values to bear on corporate life.[14] Nevertheless, philosophers (of whatever persuasion) are certainly right to claim that the moral character of the CSR debate cannot be circumvented. The amoralist approach is a dead end, because without some moral foundation we are left without the standards needed to evaluate current claims and practices. Even though there are good reasons to question the benefits of the doctrines proposed by the most vocal proponents of CSR,[15] we must not make the opposite mistake of concluding that morality has no place in evaluating corporate practices.

### C. *The Social Permission Theory*

The social permission theory tends to ground the moral foundations of CSR on the idea that society determines the nature and scope of moral obligation or responsibility. This outlook is often associated with the concession theory or the legal creator theory. Since the concession theory holds that corporations are legal entities created in the first instance by the state, the ground rules for the behavior of corporations are set by the state (through its laws). The state monitors the behavior of corporations and may legitimately alter the nature of the ground rules if the state so desires. Since corporations are created for a social purpose, they have a say in the ground rules only as a courtesy or because they have the power to influence legislation, but not because they have any rights independent of the social purpose. Corporate behavior is, thus, legitimate only to the extent that it serves this social purpose. If the needs of society change, corporations are obliged to change also.[16]

A review of the literature will indicate the strong commitment social permission theorists have to the concession theory.[17] Thus, an interesting question arises on just how dependent the social permission theory is on the concession theory. Would the social permission theory be refuted if the concession theory were shown to be false? Recently the concession theory has come under serious attack by Robert Hessen.[18] Hessen argues that corporations are not creatures of the state. Instead, the state simply recognizes what has already acquired an independent existence. An analogy can be drawn here to marriage. The state does not create the love and "corporate" unity that is the essence of marriage. The state only recognizes formally what the parties themselves have agreed upon. In a similar fashion, corporations are essentially brought into existence outside of the state and then recognized by the state.[19]

There can be little doubt that the social permission theory is seriously weakened if the concession theory turns out to be false. I do not, however, believe that the demise of the concession theory would be fatal to the social permission view. All the social permission theory needs to do if the concession theory is discarded is to claim that the corporation is a *social* creation along with marriages, states themselves, and perhaps even personalities. All institutions, and perhaps all individuals, could be viewed as social products whose behavior is legitimized by the social norms of the society from which they arose. Corporations would not be essentially legal "persons," but rather socially evolved structures which are tolerated only to the extent that they serve society. The same could be said for legal rules and institutions. Thus, the concession theory need not be taken as foundational. Nevertheless, if the concession theory were to be discarded, the social permission theory would become more of an abstract philosophy than a description of the real world.

The concession theory is not the only concept one often finds associated with the social permission theory. A common notion running through a number of the articles in a popular business ethics text is the idea that business has made a "social contract" with society at large.[20] The obligation of business to society (CSR) is thought to be found in this social contract, since all will admit that contractual relations establish obligations. For some this "contract" is an ongoing process whose terms and conditions can change, thus changing the responsibilities of business itself.[21] Those who view the social contract in this way are in danger of losing sight of the moral question and falling into the functional school; for often little more is argued for than that the times are changing and business ought to keep up.

If we focus more on the idea of a "contract," however, and less on the process of its changing terms, perhaps a more solid framework of obligations can be built. But it is worth noting that this "social contract" is a very odd contract, indeed. Apart from the fact that there is some problem in determining when such a contract was made and how such a universal contract could ever go beyond the most minimal of terms (well below what most CSR advocates desire), this "contract" seems inherently one-sided. For example, if society changes the terms of the contract, the other party (business) is not allowed to withdraw from the "agreement." One side, therefore, dictates to the other instead of there being a true contractual relation of mutual consent.[22]

This last point can be seen more fully if we examine some of the claims made by Norman Bowie.[23] Accepting the idea that business functions by social permission, Bowie seems to conclude that businesses are not only obligated to those who actually create them (owners), but also to those who permit them. The intuitive plausibility of this claim, however, is lacking. It is certainly true that I can walk the streets unmolested only because my neighbors have "permitted" me to do so by restraining their behavior. But it hardly follows from this that I have any more of an obligation to my neighbors than my own restraint in not molesting them. It certainly does not follow that I am morally obligated to take a different route simply because most of my neighbors have decided not to permit me to take the path I have chosen. If there is any "obligation," here, it would be of a "might makes right" variety.

Bowie tries to avoid the conclusion that the "social contract" between business and society amounts to little more than the will of the stronger by asking why business should submit to new terms demanding more social responsibility. Bowie offers three reasons on why business should submit to a restructuring of the social contract: 1) the "Iron Law of Responsibility" demands it; 2) if one contributes to social harm, one is obligated to rectify it; and 3) those who have the most resources should do most to correct social ills.[24] The first reason can be dismissed as not being a moral argument. It is perhaps irrelevant anyway, since if this is an actual "law" business will either respond properly or succumb to the inevitable. In either case we will not have to put up with "socially irresponsible" behavior.

The second and third reasons are meant to establish moral norms. The second reason, however, is essentially platitudinous. Few would deny that if a serious harm is done, some rectification is owed. But given all the complications in deciding what constitutes "harm,"[25] what difference there is between "harm" and "social harm," what specific cases of harm are being referred to, and why the "old" social contract was not adequate for dealing with these harms, this second reason has so little to offer that it begs all the important questions. The chief problem with the second reason, however, is not the points just mentioned, but rather that CSR most often presents itself as a positive doctrine and not the negative one of rectification. It would seem, then, that the third reason is the most significant of the three.

The third reason is no more satisfactory than the other two. If one deals honestly with others and commits no act of fraud or violence, then why does it follow that one's obligations increase as one's wealth does? The only possible answer could be that the resources attributed to business do not in fact belong to business, but rather to society at large. Business is viewed as the trustee of society's resources. Thus, however society wants those resources used, business is obligated to comply. And it is reasonable to suppose that the more resources society puts into the hands of business, the more it will care about how they are used. Notice, though, that this approach implies that when business became a party to the "contract," it did so as a trustee rather than as an owner of resources. But if this is the case, no argument is necessary, for it is obvious that trustees are obligated to carry out the wishes of the owners. Bowie, thus, needs to demonstrate that businesses are merely "trustees" of society's resources. This principle, however, cannot be demonstrated by assuming its validity. The third reason, consequently, does not so much establish an obligation as it offers a framework from which certain obligations are said to follow.

The conception of society as the owner of all resources is not, however, a framework one needs to take as given. If this principle were true, not only would businesses attain a trustee status, but also it is likely that our own personal property and even our bodily parts would not be a matter of entitlement but of permission.[26] Since society itself is conceived as a person who has "values," "interests," and "goods," as well as "resources," this theory must treat individuals as a means to some greater social end, rather than as ends in themselves. Moreover, the practical result would surely be more control over people's lives and businesses by the state in order to insure that the "interests" of society are being served.

Although some may find the implications of this version of the social permission theory sufficient grounds for its rejection, the foregoing remarks are primarily designed to identify fundamental assumptions and their implications. Quite often the assumptions go unstated, as if they were obviously true. Keith Davis, on the other hand, manages to be forthright about this matter: "the fundamental assumption...is that society has entrusted to business large amounts of society's resources to accomplish its mission, and business is expected to manage these resources as a wise trustee for society."[27] Yet by simply rejecting this assumption, much of the case for the social permission theory is rendered inert.

Some authors nevertheless have attempted to justify the foregoing assumption or one similar to it. Thomas Donaldson has recently made an effort to show why social contract theory is the best way to establish CSR.[28] Ostensibly Donaldson does not start with the assumption that business is a trustee for society's resources. Instead, Donaldson imagines a hypothetical situation for drawing up the original terms of the social contract. The terms of the contract will be whatever the two parties (business and society) can mutually agree upon. Donaldson believes that both parties will mutually consent to a number of obligations which are often only partially recognized today. These obligations include minimizing "the depletion of natural resources" and minimizing the "lack of worker control," "dehumanization," and "alienation."[29]

Unfortunately, Donaldson's attempt to justify the foundations of a social contract between business and society fails completely. Contrary to first appearances, Donaldson *does* assume that resources belong to society as a whole.[30] Since business is entitled to either few or no resources, it is obvious that the "contract" in question is at best one of trying to establish how business might function as a trustee. More probably, there is no true contract here at all. Instead, the situation seems to be that one of the parties (business) is simply waiting to be told how to behave. What bargaining power could business possibly have if it is devoid of resources? Business could not even be viewed as selling its expertise, since it could have no resources prior to the original contract upon which to demonstrate that expertise.

Secondly, Donaldson assumes that the existence of "productive organizations" needs to be justified.[31] If, however, productive organizations are the result of voluntary agreement among individuals and not designed for the purpose of undermining the possibility of voluntary agreement itself (e.g., by force), it is not at all clear why any "justification" is called for. This is especially true, paradoxically, if businesses are regarded as "individuals" as Donaldson seems to regard them. Since none of the *classical* social contract theorists (Hobbes, Locke, and Rousseau) thought it necessary to justify the actual existence of the parties to the contract itself, Donaldson should not be doing so here without explanation. Of course, if Donaldson rejects the notion that corporations are individuals in the strict sense, then the reason for using the social contract strategy would itself be jeopardized. Who, for example, would be the parties to the contract?

Finally, Donaldson holds that productive organizations are "single agents, especially in the eyes of the law."[32] Yet, if the law already recognizes productive organizations as "single agents," then it must be true that the social contract has already taken place. For unless one holds that the rules (laws) governing the behavior of individuals exist prior to the social contract itself (which would render the contract otiose), we must suppose that some contract has already taken place. But if this is so, then Donaldson's theory is really a request for an *additional* social contract; and I fail to see why business would wish to submit to an additional contract or why they should be singled out as having to do so.

Like all social permission theorists, Donaldson begins with the point of view that individuals (corporate or otherwise) are entitled to their goals and holdings only so long as those goals or holdings serve the interests of society. Indeed, Donaldson specifically states that individual rights may be sacrificed for the social good.[33] *It seems reasonable to conclude, then, that the common element running through the analyses we have discussed can be stated as follows: 1) there is a "social good" different from and superior to the goods pursued or agreed to by the individual members of society; and 2) the plans, purposes, and interests of individual members of society can be (forcibly if necessary) subordinated to the good of society as a whole.* The "proofs" most often used to justify an expanded view of CSR generally assume the perspective identified by these two components.

It would be a mistake, however, to assume that the social contract position exhausts the approaches to the social permission theory. Richard T. De George, for example, does not appeal to a social contract per se, but rather to the moral norms generated by existing social life.[34] The methodology, here, seems to be one of observing currently operative norms and then applying them to a business context. De George's approach does not essentially alter the basic components identified above; but instead of trying to deduce a set of obligations from a hypothetical contract, De George would tend to put more emphasis on actual practices, such as legal processes.[35] Since the law (and public opinion) is placing more and more demands on business, there can be little doubt that De George's theory can establish increased CSR. Nevertheless, De George's analysis is only compelling if one has already accepted as legitimate recent trends in law and morals. The critic who questions these trends seems to be dismissed out of hand. Moreover, this theory would come rather close to the functional school.

No doubt there are numerous other types of theories that could be mentioned as versions of the social permission concept. We have not, for example, discussed a utilitarian defense of CSR. A utilitarian defense of CSR would not appeal to social rules or contracts, but to the total social benefit of expanding the responsibilities of corporations. It is interesting to note, however, that although utilitarian modes of analysis are used in *applying* the concept of CSR (e.g., the corporate social audit), utilitarianism is not as common a defense of the foundations of CSR as other approaches. This could be because of the decline in the use of utilitarian arguments among moral philosophers. I suspect, though, that the reason lies elsewhere. Since business itself conducts its operations in terms of contracts, and since obligations associated with contracts are generally held to be binding, social contract theories can readily play on the sense of obligation that already exists in business. In addition, given the need for business to keep current, the functional theory or a position like De George's can appeal to business in a way that utilitarianism may not—that is, these theories can appeal to the survival instinct of a business rather than to an abstract concept like "social benefit." Finally, those businessmen who themselves see moral obligation in utilitarian terms do so from primarily an economic point of view. Yet most who argue for a strong sense of CSR want to expand the scope of moral obligations beyond the economic. Indeed, if economics is regarded as the science of maximizing social benefit, many of the proposals made to increase CSR would find opposition from economists.[36] For these reasons utilitarianism is not as common a foundation for CSR as one might expect.

The foregoing discussion does not claim to be an exhaustive analysis of all current attempts to justify CSR from a "social" point of view. The analysis does, on the other hand, claim to be reasonably accurate in identifying the basic assumptions of those demanding ever increasing social responsibility from business. Although I have tried to offer some reasons for rejecting the social permission approach, my main purpose here has been modest. CSR may, in fact, be a popular trend; but it is by no means an approach one is morally compelled to accept. Thus, since I believe the individual agreement position is both plausible and morally sound, no one, despite all the literature to the contrary, should believe that a rejection of the social permission theory is equivalent to a rejection of moral values.

# III. A Theory of Corporate Freedom and Responsibility

> The world will be redeemed; it is being redeemed. It is being redeemed not by those who shake the red rag of wordy warfare, who threaten and demand, but by its enterprisers, workers, inventors, toilers—the men and women who do the duty that lies nearest them.
>
> Elbert Hubbard
> *The Book of Business,* 1913

## A. *Friedman's Argument*

In the area of CSR, the individual agreement theory is epitomized by Milton Friedman's famous statement that, "there is one and only one social responsibility of business—to use its resources and engage in activities designed to increase its profits so long as it stays within the rules of the game, which is to say, engages in open and free competition, without deception or fraud."[1] This statement, and often the remarks from *Capitalism and Freedom* that surround it, is almost without exception reprinted in every text concerned with CSR. The contrast between Friedman's position and some of those stated in the last chapter should be evident. Yet, despite the constant criticism Friedman's argument has been subjected to, few clear and systematic presentations of that argument have been offered. The following should remedy that lack of a well defined presentation of Friedman's position.[2]

Friedman's argument seems to depend on an assumption that can be stated in either a weak (hypothetical) or strong (categorical) form. The weak version would be: if we want to maintain a capitalist society, the sanctity of the contract must remain inviolable (deception and fraud violate that sanctity). The strong version might read: there is no morally legitimate reason to call for the violation of contractual relationships for the sake of some other social good which is not itself necessary for the very existence of social order. Whether one picks the strong or weak version, it is clear that the sanctity of the contract represents a strong moral commitment. Given this commitment, Friedman's argument would have two basic parts and would run as follows:

The Profit Maximization Argument

1. Corporate managers are fiduciaries of the corporate owners (e.g., stockholders).
2. Corporate owners have only one interest in and reason for hiring managers—to maximize profits.
3. Therefore, corporate managers would violate their fiduciary trust by engaging in actions that are unrelated to (or which consciously minimize) profit maximization.

The Social Responsibility Argument

4. Acts of corporate charity ("social responsibility") lessen the amount of profits the firm and/or owners receive.
5. If corporate managers act in ways described in #4, they would violate their contractual responsibilities to owners. (by #3)
6. A call for managers to be "socially responsible" is a call for them to violate their contractual obligations. (by #4 and 5)
7. Thus, managers should not direct their firms into "socially responsible" activities.

If one returns to Friedman's statement quoted above, it is clear that the foregoing argument addresses the issue of why a corporation's sole responsibility is profit maximization. This argument does not, however, defend or explain that part of the statement that speaks of "the rules of the game" or "open and free competition." More on this in a moment.

In contrast to the social permission theory, the foregoing argument suggests that Friedman believes corporations to be collections of individuals who have pooled resources to which they are entitled into an organization whose purpose is to make a profit. Thus, the corporation is not an end in itself, nor is it an essentially public institution despite the large numbers of persons who may be associated with it. If the resources are privately held by the individuals who form the corporation, then the act of pooling or investing does not transform those assets into public assets simply because large numbers participate. It would seem to follow, then, that corporations are not creatures of the state, but are, rather, private institutions whose existence is recognized by law.

There are, nevertheless, ambiguities in Friedman's argument. The most obvious ambiguity is that the concept of "profit maximization" is not given a time frame. Whether profits are to be made over the short or long term may make a difference in a corporation's behavior. Yet although this issue may affect behavior, it does not affect the fundamentals of the CSR debate. For the whole point of Friedman's critics is to show that there is something above, beyond, or in spite of profit seeking that corporations must consider. These critics cannot claim that profit seeking and "social responsibility" are consistent and still remain critics. Thus, the short term/long term question might be relevant within the context Friedman lays down, but not between Friedman and his opponents.[3]

One might also wish to question the assumption (proposition #2) that corporate owners seek to maximize profits. It could be suggested that the owners do not seek to maximize, but rather wish only a certain rate of return. Provided one is not required to interpret "maximize" to mean what would be received if all parties had perfect information, this question need not detain us either. As long as there is competition for the investment dollar, corporate managers would be obligated by Friedman's argument to make their company as attractive an investment opportunity as possible. If certain managers acted otherwise, funds would tend to flow away from that corporation. This outflow of funds would threaten the firm's ability to meet the "less-than-maximal-return" expected by the original investors.

There are, however, some ambiguities in Friedman's argument that cannot be dismissed so easily. In the first place, there is some vagueness about what Friedman means by the "rules of the game" and "open and free competition." Presumably these questions are meant to be clarified to some extent by not allowing "deception and fraud." Yet even this degree of clarification does not show why "deception and fraud" are given such a central role or why other values should not also be given equal weight. Thus, Friedman's argument would seem to need a broader and firmer ethical foundation to provide the context within which his CSR argument would function. Secondly, Friedman's argument does not preclude the pursuit of moral goals—only the pursuit of those goals at the expense of profitability. Furthermore, there is some question here as to whether morality and profitability are necessarily in conflict. It may be possible to see morality and profit-seeking as being compatible and mutually interdependent concepts. Friedman's argument may, therefore, allow for the inclusion of some concerns that have been pushed by advocates of opposing theories of CSR.

The two categories of ambiguities just mentioned can serve as questions to be answered in the remaining pages of this chapter. With respect to the first issue, it is my belief that a theory of individual rights provides the needed context for Friedman's argument.[4] And although a full justification for such a theory of rights cannot be provided here, I can outline the main features of that theory and show how those features provide the context needed to explain, for example, why a company has an "obligation to pay its debts...even if its 'exclusive' duty is to make as much money as possible."[5] The question of profitability and morality will, then, be treated descriptively later in this chapter.

## B. *Individual Rights*

The theory of rights being proposed here is a theory of individual "natural" or "human" rights. Natural or human rights are rights possessed by persons in virtue of their being persons and not by virtue of considerations of the consequences of a person's actions or contractual arrangements. Thus, to be a human person is sufficient grounds for claiming such rights. Although many different types of justifications have been used to explain these rights,[6] all agree that individuals are in an important sense "ends in themselves." On this theory, to be an "end in oneself" means that no one's purposes are subservient to or a means to the purposes of other individuals or groups. Each person is free to pursue his or her own ends provided those ends do not prevent others from being able to formulate purposes of their own.[7] The initiation of physical force by one person (or group) against another is the most significant form of removing the other's ability to formulate plans and goals of his own.[8] Thus, no person (or group) may use force against others in achieving his own ends.

Rights express the necessary moral "side constraints" on an individual's (or group's) behavior. These side constraints represent the broadest possible boundaries within which an individual is entitled to act without encroaching on another's "moral space." The boundaries themselves are set by the principle of the non-initiation of physical force. Thus, one is entitled to pursue whatever goals one desires provided one does not cross another's moral boundaries by the initiation of force. It is important to notice that what one has a right to do may not always be what is right. I may, for example, have every right to gamble away my earnings at the race track even though (by some additional moral standard) it may not be right that I do so.[9] Thus, what one is entitled to do may not always be what one ought to do. Certainly this idea is not without intuitive plausibility.[10]

One person obviously initiates force (coerces) another (and thus violates the other's rights) when that person physically assaults another person. Moreover, one's rights are violated when one is threatened with such actions, for it is only reasonable to assume that the threats are seriously intended. These rights establish that persons are entitled to their own personhood, which means their bodies and minds. And since persons are material beings who must act by extending themselves into the material world, attacks upon extensions of a person (property) are attacks upon persons themselves. That is why such actions as theft and extortion violate a person's rights. For our purposes, however, the most significant form of rights violations is the various types of fraud (contractual violations). If one person does not live up to the terms of a contract or fraudulantly enters into a contractual relationship, the other party can claim a rights violation. Such acts are rights violating because they destroy the foundation of mutual consent upon which voluntary (as opposed to coercive) relationships depend. The non-consensual behavior of the rights violator in this case is, also, true of the other rights violations mentioned before.

The only way, therefore, to insure that a person's interests in his own resources are respected is to enlist that person's consent. Since coercion is to be banned from human relationships, mutual agreement or consent becomes the necessary standard for determining rights respecting actions. Thus, if the resources of one person were coercively expropriated to enhance the resources or circumstances of another, the first person would become a means to the ends of another. This is one reason why individual rights are essentially "negative." Individuals must refrain from crossing the boundaries of others. "Positive" rights, which require the taking of the resources of some for the benefit of others, treat the ends of some persons as more significant than the ends of others. Indeed, it is virtually impossible to maintain a system of individual rights if one admits the existence of positive rights; for in order to insure that the welfare claims of some are fulfilled, resources must be taken from others without their consent.

From this brief outline of the major features of a theory of individual rights, one can see why Friedman's argument legitimately places such emphasis on respecting contractual agreements and eschews force, fraud, and deception. Corporations (being groups of individuals) would have the same obligations to respect individual rights as individuals have among each other. And it is because of this theory of individual rights that corporations cannot employ acts of violence, fraud, or deception against consumers or competitors. This theory of individual rights also explains why employees of a corporation must live up to their contract with the owners not to sacrifice profits. Traditional examples of management abuse of this fiduciary trust include divulging company secrets, maintaining an interest in a competing firm, using company resources for unauthorized personal gain, and the like. By the same token, however, it would violate the rights of those persons who are the owners of a corporation to require (e.g., by government dictate) that some of their resources be used to "cure social ills." Thus, we might modify Friedman's principle by claiming that the only universally obligatory "social responsibility" a corporation has is to respect individual rights—rather than, as Friedman puts it, to "increase profits."[11]

### C. *The False Dichotomy Between Morality and Profits*

It has been common in business ethics texts to render Friedman's argument as essentially an economic one. Thus, the student is usually given the "choice" of either adopting an economic outlook or one that includes human (e.g., moral) values. Consider this representative sample:

> If society wants to maximize economic efficiency and productivity, then perhaps there will be less risk if business stays away from social involvement. On the other hand, if social and human values are of major importance to society, then perhaps business should move toward more social involvement...[12]

Obviously a passage such as this one identifies moral values with the second alternative offered. Moreover, the passage implies that objections to CSR are all economically motivated. It is, thus, especially important to notice that Friedman's argument is essentially a moral argument and not an economic one.[13] And when the individual rights theory is used to further strengthen Friedman's argument, the moral character of the argument is even more easily recognized. As I noted at the end of the last chapter, a rejection of the usual arguments for CSR is by no means the same as a rejection of moral values.[14]

The dichotomy often drawn between profits and morality is not a correct one. Under the version of the individual agreement theory just described, profits and morality are necessarily related because management's pursuit of profits fulfills management's obligation to the owners. Nevertheless, a corporation that is conscientious about respecting individual rights (by living up to contractual obligations) may still face moral issues. Unfortunately, Friedman's argument suggests: 1) it is evident which courses of action will enhance or detract from profits, and thus 2) the obligation to maximize profits severely limits the courses of action open to responsible management. If these interpretations turn out to be questionable, then corporations may have more flexibility in satisfying their prime obligation to maximize profits than appears on the surface. Yet whatever else a corporation should consider, the theory presented above requires that profitability not be sacrificed in the process.

The question of what will enhance a corporation's profitability is not unambiguous. There is, first of all, the issue of long run versus short run profitability. Friedman's argument does not address which one of these two strategies is meant by "maximizing profits." Perhaps Friedman's argument is best formulated without an answer to this question, since in a free market there would likely be a wide variety of corporate attitudes on profitability. Indeed, one would expect to find as divergent a set of corporate attitudes as one finds varying degrees of present or future orientation among individuals. And just as we might recommend to individuals to look to the long run, so we might also make such a recommendation to management. Yet it is also true that we show our respect for others by not interfering with their ultimate responsibility for deciding just how long or short run their thinking will be in certain circumstances and under certain conditions. Likewise, divergent strategies for return on equity may reflect different circumstances, abilities, and knowledge on the part of both investors and managers. Thus, policies could be responsible under either a long or short term attitude.

It does seem reasonable to suppose that what many call "socially responsible" behavior would more likely be achieved by long run rather than short run attitudes by corporate executives. Yet it also seems quite unreasonable to determine *a priori* that all must operate under a universalized normative rule to maximize in the long term. And it seems equally unreasonable to suggest that a certain course of action is necessarily profit minimizing under any and all circumstances. The ambiguity in Friedman's argument allows for diversity on these matters. Some policies might seem rather narrowly focused and yet be the most responsible course of action under the circumstances. But some policies which look "socially responsible" may, thus, be quite consistent with profitability in the long run.

An example of the last point might be the actions of William C. Norris of Control Data Corporation. Norris believes that, "technology exists to solve society's major problems. The company that can do that will be the company of the future." And he has further stated that, "Social problems provide profit-making opportunities."[15] Norris has decided to devote corporate resources in the "inner city" and elsewhere for the purpose of creating learning centers. These learning centers, containing CDC products, are meant to develop entrepreneurial skills that could make regular customers out of those who become successful and who are accustomed to using CDC products. As *Business Week* put it:

> While that might sound like lip service to social responsibility, that is not the case at CDC. Norris already has bet at least $300 million in trying to position Control Data for leadership in a wide range of socially oriented markets, especially in education and training.[16]

Obviously it is too early to tell whether Norris' strategy will pay off. But the fact that he has undertaken this project indicates the wide range of options open to "profit seekers."

Another ambiguity inherent in the idea of profitability is whether the factors contributing to profits are to be exclusively quantitative. For the most part the world of business is properly a world of "facts and figures." Yet qualitative elements such as image, personal relations, good will, etc., are factors that can have an impact on profitability in ways that are not easily quantifiable. The ways in which any of these factors (quantitative or qualitative) affect a corporation should be assessed at the time. It is, again, unreasonable to expect to universalize rules to correctly decide such factors in specific cases. For some businesses, the qualitative factors may be more significant than in other businesses (e.g., service industries may be more sensitive to image than manufacturing firms). It would, therefore, be difficult to exclude *a priori* almost any action as being a necessary detriment to profitability in all cases.

Just as Friedman's opponents make the mistake of supposing that there is a list of "socially responsible" policies that all businesses must recognize, so also does Friedman assume that there are some acts inherently detrimental to profitability. Charitable contributions (specifically to universities) are listed by Friedman as being profit reducing.[17] To make such categorical assertions would require one to suppose that there are no realistically imaginable circumstances under which such contributions would enhance the qualitative factors that may improve corporate profitability. Past experience has not been kind to those who make categorical pronouncements about the profit minimizing nature of certain courses of action. For example, in 1914 Ford Motor Company increased its wages to $5 a day and reduced the work day from 9 to 8 hours. This policy was not viewed at the time as good business, but as virtually an act of charity. Indeed, the *Wall Street Journal* commented that, "this [policy] is on a high biblical or spiritual principle where [it does] not belong."[18] It may be better to let the market decide whether quality circles, Scanlon plans, participatory management, corporate charity drives, rehabilitation programs, and the like are fads or ultimate profit enhancers, than it would be to listen to either Friedman or Nader tell us what is or is not "profit maximizing" or "socially responsible."[19]

Having rejected the idea that certain actions are intrinsically profit reducing or socially responsible ("1" above), it now remains for us to question the false dichotomy between profits and morality. My argument will not be that profits and moral values can never conflict, nor that seeking profits can never tempt one to forget about moral values. Instead, I wish to object to the idea that if one accepts the modified version of Friedman's argument (discussed above) one must see moral values as merely a means to profitability without any value in their own right. If, for example, a corporation is considering installing a program for alcohol rehabilitation, there are those who will argue for such a program because it is "morally right" irrespective of profitability; and there are, also, those who will argue that there is no other value to be considered than the impact on corporate productivity and profits. A manager faced with these two recommendations would seem to be given a choice between moral actions which reduce profits and amoral actions which maintain them.

A manager need not, however, see his or her moral values as either overriding or subservient to profitability. It is possible for a person to regard his moral values both as goods that have value in their own right and as goods that have value because they contribute to some other end. This possibility is suggested by some recent work on Aristotle concerning his conception of the nature of means and ends.[20] If we first give a very brief summary of how Aristotle's theory could apply to an individual's own plans, we can then apply the lesson to a corporate context.

Aristotle held that it is possible for there to be something which is an end in itself and not merely a means to some other end. Some have felt that if there is an end in itself, then other ends that people pursue and which are not this particular end in itself could have value *only* because of their contribution to this particular end. For example, if happiness[21] is an end in itself (and this was Aristotle's own position), then other values must be a means to that end and could not be considered as having value as ends in their own right. The problem with such a view is that other ends people pursue *do* seem to have value quite apart from their contribution to that which is said to be an "end in itself." For example, if happiness is an end in itself, it does not seem true to say that (e.g.) justice has merely instrumental value with respect to happiness—that is, justice is valuable only because of what it contributes to happiness. Justice seems to have value in its own right, whatever its contribution to happiness. By the same token, if justice is said to be an end in itself, it is not true to say that ends like pleasure or friendship have their own value only to the extent that they contribute something to justice. One finds in Aristotle a way out of saying that something can only be either a means to an end or an end in itself.

In order to remove the purely instrumental quality of some values, it must be possible to have ends which can both contribute to another end and also be activities valued for their own sake. Suppose, for example, that I choose to have a good vacation. Suppose I also regard friendship to be "its own reward." Given these values I may plan my vacation to include frequent visits or conversations with my friends. It would be correct to say that visits with my friends are a means to having a good vacation. But it would also be correct to say that these visits have value apart from their contribution to my vacation. Moreover, it would be incorrect to say that I am just using my friends as a means to having a good vacation, even though my conversations with them contribute to that end. Thus, the value of friendship need not be lessened by its contribution to some other end.

If we apply a similar kind of reasoning to corporate decisions, we may obtain a similar result. Suppose there is a manager committed to his responsibility of maximizing profits and also committed to fair and harmonious relations with his employees. This manager is, furthermore, considering whether his company should finance rehabilitation programs for employees with an alcohol problem. In his research he discovers that it would be less expensive (or equally expensive) to finance this program than it would be to fire the employees and retrain new ones. Moreover, he believes that instituting such a program would enhance prospects for better employees in the future. He, therefore, installs the program feeling that he has made a morally correct choice in terms of both profitability and human relations. In this case, it would certainly be inaccurate to claim that the manager only *really* cares about profits and not about his employees. The manager may, however, find out that the program was too expensive given his company's marginal market position. Firing or laying off alcoholic employees would then be his chosen course of action. In this latter case too it would be quite unreasonable to conclude that this manager cares only about the "bottom line" and not about the welfare or special problems of his employees.

The foregoing example shows why many managers rightly resent the implication that any morally worthy action consistent with profitability must reduce one value to the other. They do not see themselves (or have to see themselves) as only caring about the "bottom line." Nor would they feel comfortable in sacrificing profits for the sake of some end they have been told is morally appropriate. If the theory proposed here is correct, moral values can be integrated with profitability without having to claim that the former derive their value only because of their contribution to the latter.[22] It is also quite important, however, not to lose sight of the fact that the pursuit of profits is itself a moral value.

Some may still object that managers do not have the degree of flexibility and range of options open to them that my remarks above suggest. After all, managers are hired by the owners (e.g., stockholders) to take those actions necessary to increase profits. Thus, managers should simply follow the wishes of the owners, and that does not seem to leave much room for choice on the part of management. Moreover, the classical theory of the firm holds that managers are *in fact* always pursuing profits, which leaves little room for other considerations. While these arguments may have substance in the context of closely held corporations, the picture is not so clear in large publicly traded companies.

Recent economic literature has suggested that as ownership becomes more diffuse, the ability of stockholders to monitor management lessens.[23] The "down side" of this phenomenon is that managers have more freedom to divert resources away from stockholders and towards themselves. But the CSR debate as it is now discussed is not concerned with this problem. Thus, for our purposes, this phenomenon of modern corporate ownership indicates that management does have a degree of flexibility unavailable to managers of the past. This is not to say that the profitability of the firm is no longer a constraint on the behavior of managers, or even to claim that profitability is a weak constraint. Rather, management now has a wider range of options to consider in judging the best course towards the profitability of the firm. Moral values may enter into the management equation without necessarily detracting from the profitability of the firm (because they are part of a package of options) and without necessarily being contrary to the wishes of the owners (since the wishes of the owners are less than precise). The market is still the final test of success, but management's choice of paths to that success is now more open.

Up to this point I have attempted to make three basic claims: *1) Friedman's conception of CSR is essentially a moral argument, especially when that argument is framed within a theory of individual rights; 2) although profitability cannot be legitimately sacrificed, the phrase "maximizing profits" is sufficiently ambiguous to allow for a variety of strategies, some of which may be "socially responsible;" and 3) one need not see his or her actions as requiring the subordination of morality to profits or vice versa.* These three themes are, nevertheless, descriptive in nature. We are still in need of some normative guidelines that can be applied to specific cases. It is to that task that I now turn.

### D. *Guidelines for Responsible Behavior*

In the preceding section I discussed a theory of CSR based upon individual rights. In the next chapter I shall apply some of the implications of that theory to concrete cases. Yet before we can look at actual proposals, it is necessary to state some of the normative principles that follow from what was said above. It is clear that one of these principles must be that no corporation can legitimately violate the rights of another person or group. It is also clear from our earlier remarks that little else of a universal and categorical nature can be said about corporate behavior. Of course, included in this principle of respecting individual rights is the idea that if the owners of a corporation are profit seekers, then managers are obligated to pursue the interests of the owners. Anything less would be rights violating. But this statement only speaks of the obligations of managers to owners and not of managers and owners towards others such as the public at large. Certainly managers and owners cannot institute policies that violate the rights of others; but we have not yet said much about what such violations look like in practice. Part of that problem will be remedied in the following chapters. For now, let us entitle this principle the *"principle of respect for individual rights."* This principle, and the other two that follow, can be used not only to evaluate corporate behavior, but also to evaluate the recommendations made by corporate critics.

Another theme discussed in the preceding sections dealt with the central role profitability played in the nature and purpose of corporations. We saw that the pursuit of profits was not merely a desire people had, but also a possible source of obligation. From this it follows that any recommendation for a course of action, other than the recommendation to respect basic rights, must consider the impact of that recommendation on profitability. This *"principle of responsible recommendation"* is often ignored by those fond of making categorical assertions about what corporations ought or ought not do, as we shall see below. This principle tends to be followed more often by those within a corporate context or who are familiar with the nature of business than by those outside of a business environment. In addition, the principle of responsible recommendation has the corollary that the benefit of the doubt be given to the one most familiar with the circumstances of a case. A recommendation cannot be responsible if it assumes beforehand that the judgment of the one to whom the recommendation is made is not worthy of respect.

Another implication of what was said in the last section is that managers have a degree of flexibility in pursuing the overall goals of the corporation. Provided that the two principles just mentioned are not at issue, this degree of flexibility imposes upon managers the responsibility to take moral values seriously. In other words, because management has a range of legitimate options to consider in formulating corporate policy, their choice of options is subject to moral evaluation (if applicable) as well as evaluation according to the principles of sound business management. As we noted in the first chapter, a person who accepts a position where decisions must be made among a variety of alternatives can be evaluated from a number of perspectives, including the moral perspective. Part of the "moral perspective" is handled by our preceding principles. What remains is an attitude of showing respect for others by considering their interests and the affects of one's policies on those interests. Thus, if one has a choice between two policies both of which are in accord with the preceding two principles, then one should consider the impact of each policy upon the interests and circumstances of those affected by the policy. If one can minimize any adverse impact while still remaining true to the prime obligations stated by the preceding principles, then one should do so.

In practice, taking moral values seriously means always being open to the moral dimension that is a part of one's actions. The person who fails to consider the interests or values of others has in effect closed off the moral dimension by behaving as if the only standard in question is the one actually used to solve the problem at hand. Being open to moral values does not mean that one must agree with what any self-proclaimed moralist might insist is the right course of action. Nor does it mean that one can take no actions that might adversely affect the interests of others. Indeed, it may be the case that what one *should* do is quite the opposite of what many claim is the correct course of action. It may, for example, be appropriate to lay off workers during a business slump. This certainly affects some people's interests adversely, but if the manager(s) a) considered the interests of others, and b) sought alternatives (consistent with our first two principles) that would minimize adverse impact, then his actions would be in accord with this third principle. Thus, the principle being advocated, here, is an attitudinal principle—not a behavioral principle. This principle, which could be entitled the "*principle of moral consideration*," sees the first two principles as primary, but recognizes that diverse circumstances and contexts faced by management may call for some additional thought about the impact of corporate policy. It should not be forgotten, however, that this same principle of moral consideration applies to those who criticize corporate policy. This is especially true if the critic presents himself as an impartial guardian of moral values, but makes no effort to consider *all* the values and interests involved in a certain issue.

We now have three basic principles that can be used to evaluate the actions of corporations and their critics and defenders. To summarize: *1) no action should be taken which violates another's individual rights; 2) recommendations must be responsible in the sense that they do not ignore the context, purpose, and basic contractual commitments of those to whom the recommendation is made; and 3) the moral dimensions of an action should always be given serious attention.* With these three basic normative principles in mind, let us turn to some concrete cases of recommendations that have been made on how corporations should behave.

# IV. South Africa

> The necessity to protect the Africans from the 'wolves,' the white capitalists, has been emphasised by spokesmen for *apartheid.* There is a familiar, contemporary ring about the catch-phrases used to justify a policy which permits only such forms of material progress as the state finds expedient....But are not the wiser social critics those who perceive that the fundamental injustice suffered by the Africans originates in those hindrances to private investment which have condemned them as a whole to avoidable backwardness, ignorance, illiteracy, poverty and high mortality. *W. H. Hutt, Economist*

A good place to examine some specific proposals for corporate social responsibility is with a recent publication of the Interfaith Center on Corporate Responsibility.[1] The Interfaith Center exists "to serve the common needs of member church agencies in their corporate responsibility programs."[2] One of the activities pursued by the various church groups is to offer proxy resolutions on corporate policies these groups feel are socially irresponsible. The Interfaith Center's publication is a lengthy collection of proxy resolutions by various member groups.

Even though such groups own relatively few shares of stock in the corporations to which they are submitting resolutions, and even though such resolutions are almost always overwhelmingly defeated, the submission of proxy resolutions remains a legitimate way for owners to express their concerns about corporate policy. The objections expressed below are thus not directed at the means employed by these groups. It should be noticed, however, that a reasonable suspicion might exist that some of these groups have purchased a few shares of stock primarily for the purpose of protesting corporate policy. If this is the case, such groups would be owners with no interest in or concern for the health and welfare of the corporation. And although it is very difficult to determine with any certainty that some have invested only with the intention to protest, if that were the motive, the other owners could legitimately ignore the protesters. Mere acts of protest would constitute a version of deception, since by buying shares these groups are presenting themselves as interested in the welfare of the corporation while in fact having no such interest.

Over 100 resolutions are listed in the Interfaith Center's publication. The vast majority of these fall into three categories: 1) South Africa, 2) nuclear technology, and 3) public utilities. The last two categories pose some special problems because of the currently quasi-public nature of these enterprises. I shall, therefore, concentrate my attention in this chapter and the ones that follow on resolutions that affect strictly private corporations. However, in order not to completely ignore problems raised by quasi-public corporations, I shall discuss nuclear technology in Chapter Eight.

### A. *Investments in South Africa*

The reason ostensibly given for objecting to corporations doing business in South Africa is that these corporations are in some way contributing to the continuation of apartheid. Apartheid violates human rights, and it is the concern for human rights that is supposed to motivate the protesting church groups. It is interesting to note, however, that although there are many resolutions against doing business in South Africa, there are no resolutions protesting corporate activities in such countries as the Soviet Union, China, Hungary, Tanzania, and the like. One would have expected church groups seriously interested in the protection of human rights to be concerned about all such violations. Some resolutions do express concern over doing business in Chile and Guatemala, but these countries are placed by church groups in the same ideological space as South Africa.

If we ignore the questionable objectivity with which these church groups express their moral outrage, the South Africa issue breaks down into three categories. The first category consists in protests against any form of trade, investment, or expansion of facilities in South Africa. The second category would include those resolutions that demand adherence to what are called "Sullivan principles." Finally, a number of resolutions have protested the selling of equipment or the making of loans to the South African government. Some groups would, of course, protest on all three counts at the same time. But few actual resolutions are so broad as to include all three categories in a single proposal. The proxy resolutions that were submitted tend to fit into one category at a time.

Within the first category, a typical proxy resolution runs as follows:

> General Electric and its subsidiaries shall make no further investment nor expand operations in South Africa, including its Bantustans, until the government commits itself to ending apartheid and takes meaningful steps toward the achievement of full political, legal and social rights for the majority of the population.[3]

This resolution, like all others, is surrounded by "supporting statements" which describe the racial policies in South Africa. Some supporting statements (such as the one connected with the GE resolution) also try to offer reasons why it might not be financially prudent to expand in a country with the potential for political instability. The factual remarks contained in these supporting statements seem accurate enough that we need not devote time to their analysis.

Instead, let us apply the three guiding principles mentioned in Chapter Three to this resolution. It is clear that if this resolution were legitimately adopted by the owners of the corporation, no one's rights would be violated. But what if the resolution is defeated. Would expansion and further investment violate anyone's rights? The answer to this question must, also, be "no," despite the common imputation that merely doing business in South Africa constitutes collusion with and support for apartheid policies. It does not follow from the fact that a government violates people's rights that a corporation doing business under that government is violating someone's rights. Moreover, a corporation which obeys the laws of the country is not necessarily a supporter of those laws. Corporations no more contribute to rights violations by their mere presence than do journalists who, for their own gain and/or pursuit of their own objectives, obey the law as they cover stories in South Africa.

It is true that if every corporation withdrew from South Africa or refused to make any further investments, the South African government would be adversely affected. It is by no means clear, however, whether the response to such actions would be more or less repression by the government. Indeed, given the fact that there have been corporations and banks that have withdrawn or limited their investments, and given the continuation of apartheid, there is little reason to expect that limiting or withdrawing investments is an effective strategy. It could even be argued that more expansion might tend to have a liberating effect upon the society.[4] In any case, there is enough ambiguity in terms of effects, that the best case one can make morally for these types of resolutions are that they are "judgment calls."

But perhaps the argument is that, regardless of effects, this whole question is a matter of principle—that is, principled people would protest such policies. This argument is in many respects weaker than the one from effects. Unless equally attractive investment alternatives are suggested, it would violate the rights of owners to sacrifice profits for the sake of making a social protest. This may seem like a choice between two principles, one of pursuing profits and the other of protecting justice. Many would like to present the issue in just this way, for when put in these terms the choice is clear. Nevertheless, the correct way to describe the alternatives, here, is whether to refuse to act in rights violating ways (by resisting demands that managers ignore their contractual obligations) or to make a social protest. Clearly, the former alternative is morally superior.

But the alternatives just mentioned (between the observation of rights and social protest) are not necessarily in conflict. If equally attractive investments were available, managers of a corporation could make both a protest and respect rights.[5] This leads us to the principle of responsible recommendation. A definitive sign of an irresponsible recommendation is one that a) fails to consider the nature and purpose of the organization (or person) in question, and b) proposes a course of action that is inconsistent or not integrated with the nature and purpose of the organization. Thus, it is essential that any recommendation concern itself first and foremost with the hazards of continued or expanded investment or the benefits of divestiture of existing investments. The proxy proposals contained in the publication in question quite often proceed as if the purpose of the corporation were irrelevant, and they almost always recommend courses of action as if the impact of remaining alternatives on the welfare of the corporation did not matter.

The proxy resolution submitted to the Perkin-Elmer corporation is an excellent example of a completely irresponsible resolution. The GE proposal that we have been examining is slightly more responsible. The GE proposal at least points to possible long term investment problems due to social instability in South Africa. I say "slightly" more responsible, since the reason given for questioning the soundness of continued investment seems more like an afterthought than a part of the core motivation. In fact, the supporting statement in the GE proposal actually contradicts itself. In one part of it the authors say that "apartheid shows no sign of breaking down" while in another part they speak of "South Africa's inherent long-term instability." The authors have simply tossed in the investment argument as bait on the hook.

By our third principle, managers should show some sensitivity and concern for doing business in countries that violate rights, even if it is their right to do business in such countries. But by the same token, these protesting groups ought to show an awareness of the nature, purpose, and obligations inherent in corporate activity. One finds little of this in the entire document published by the Interfaith Center. Indeed, one finds so little appreciation of and respect for corporate activity in these proposals, that one is tempted to conclude that ideology rather than moral concern moves these church groups.

A responsible recommendation that showed awareness of the nature of business activity would attempt to integrate the particular moral concern with the general purpose of the corporation and with the specific circumstances of the particular corporation. It is not impossible (or perhaps even difficult) to think of sound reasons why the apartheid environment may not be a good one for further investment, just as there are possible reasons for not investing in socialist or communist countries. And with respect to South Africa, there have been corporations which have apparently discovered such reasons.[6] Thus, unless the corporation is engaging in rights violating actions, the first concern of a responsible proxy resolution must be the welfare of the corporation. That welfare may also be quite consistent with other moral concerns.

## B. *The Sullivan Principles*

It would seem that by the principle of moral consideration resolutions in favor of the Sullivan Principles would be the proper course of action for a corporation to follow with respect to South Africa. The Sullivan Principles were developed by Dr. Leon Sullivan, a Baptist minister who sits on the board of General Motors. They were designed to specify "minimum desegregation and fair employment standards for American corporations operating in South Africa."[7] There are six "principles" which run as follows:

1. Nonsegregation of the races in all eating, comfort and work facilities.

2. Equal and fair employment practices for all employees (including non-discriminatory benefit plans).
3. Equal pay for all employees doing comparable work (including an equitable system of job classification).
4. Instituting training programs which will prepare substantial numbers of blacks for supervisory, administrative, clerical and technical jobs.
5. Increasing the number of blacks in management and supervisory positions.
6. Improving the quality of employee's lives outside the workplace in areas such as housing, transportation, schooling, recreation and health facilities.

According to one proxy resolution, over 135 United States corporations have subscribed to the Sullivan Principles.[8] Subscribing corporations include IBM, Exxon, General Motors, Mobil, Ford, and General Electric. According to the Interfaith Center publication, corporations being petitioned to subscribe to the Sullivan Principles include American Home Products, Ingersoll-Rand, Dun & Bradstreet, and Dresser Industries.

Here is the resolution directed at American Home Products:

> That American Home Products shall sign and take steps to implement the Sullivan Principles. In the event that American Home Products South African subsidiary has not complied, by December 31, 1983, with each of the six Sullivan Principles, the corporation shall take whatever steps are necessary to terminate its South African operations.[9]

The latter part of this resolution clearly violates the principle of responsible recommendation, since it demands divestiture without presenting workable alternatives. Let us, therefore, concentrate on the demand to simply implement the Sullivan Principles.

Given the theory advanced in this paper, no corporation is morally required to act in accordance with the sixth principle. In and of itself, this principle is simply a call for the redistribution of wealth, and wealth cannot be redistributed in this way without the permission of the owners.[10] The fifth principle, which makes no mention of merit or marginal productivity to the firm, is simply a call to promote on the basis of race. Hence, the fifth principle is, at best, of dubious moral value. The fourth principle shares some of the problems of the fifth, but at least it supposes that training will contribute to the welfare of the firm. Depending on how these training programs are undertaken, the fourth principle could be acceptable.

The third principle advocates adopting the "equal pay for comparable work" concept. As we shall see in another chapter, this concept is so filled with logical difficulties that no one could reasonably be obligated to support it. In a general sense, however, the "equal pay for comparable work" concept is an attempt to replace market determination of wages with a system of *a priori* bureaucratic rules. The second Sullivan principle is either vacuous or defined by the other five principles. The first principle seems reasonable enough, provided the corporation can do these things without punitive action from the government.

It is clear from this discussion that the Sullivan Principles cannot be as unqualifiedly endorsed as its supporters claim. Moreover, as a whole the Sullivan Principles represent the kind of abstract and context independent rules that, I have been arguing, ignore the responsibilities to which managers have contractually committed themselves. Nevertheless, as a call for attitudinal sensitivity to racial problems, the Sullivan Principles (in this restricted sense) could accord with our own third principle. But as I have also noted, many of the specifics associated with the Sullivan Principles violate our principle of responsible recommendation.

### C. *Business and the South African Government*

The situation is somewhat different when it comes to doing business directly with the South African government. Since the government is directly involved in rights violations, the question becomes one of whether U.S. companies doing business with the government can be directly implicated in those violations.[11] It is important to realize, however, that it has been illegal since 1978 for corporations to deal directly with the South African military or police. Presumably, this law was passed to insure that U.S. corporations would not be direct participants in the violation of human rights. I shall operate below with this law as a given and not question the wisdom of the law itself.

Given the existence of the 1978 law, the kinds of proposals one finds in the Interfaith Center's publication break down into three basic categories. First of all, some proposals (e.g., to Motorola) demand a resolution against doing business with the South African military or police in case the U.S. eases its restrictions in this matter. Secondly, some proposals (e.g., Control Data and Sperry) ask for monitoring the sale of products to insure that none of them (especially computers) get into the hands of the South African military or police. Finally, some proposals (e.g., to Westinghouse) urge divestiture or the limitation of any further investments in projects connected with the South African government even though the investment is unrelated to military or police activities (in this case a coal gasification system).[12]

In an example like the Motorola case, these kinds of proxy proposals seem to have the purpose of using the corporation as a vehicle for social protest. Since the 1978 law is in force, there is no need to urge the company to refrain from doing business with the South African military or police. In effect, then, the protesters are asking the corporation to devote current time and resources to a matter unrelated to present activities. One must conclude, therefore, that the purpose behind such a resolution is to make a social statement. But surely such protest is beyond the purpose of the corporation and the interests of most of its owners. Consequently, there is no obligation to consider such a proposal, and time would be better spent pursuing matters that directly affect business operations.

The second example (Control Data and Sperry) seems like a call for insuring obedience to the law. In fact, however, this kind of proposal violates the principle of responsible recommendation. In general, if a corporation were knowingly and willingly selling goods to a government that is buying them solely because they are efficient tools in violating rights, then there would, indeed, be a moral difficulty. But to say that is a long way from saying that the corporation is obligated to monitor all the various paths and uses its products take after they have been sold. For the most part, corporations cannot be held responsible if their products are used in immoral ways after they are sold. Furthermore, these proposals make no reference to the costs of monitoring the uses to which their products are put. There is little doubt that such monitoring procedures are likely to be quite expensive, especially because there is no limit in principle to how long a corporation would have to monitor the paths its products have taken. Such proxy resolutions violate our principle of responsible recommendation by ignoring the impact on the welfare of the corporation.

Finally, there are cases where businesses are engaged in projects with the South African government that are not directly connected to the military or police (e.g., Westinghouse's coal gasification system). Since most countries consider it a proper function of government to control or "own" public utilities, the Westinghouse example seems to be in the same category as our earlier examples of strictly private operations in South Africa and should be evaluated in the same manner. It is not because Westinghouse is working with coal gasification that it is being subjected to this proxy proposal, but because it is doing so in South Africa. As we noted above, the mere fact that a company is doing business in South Africa is not a sufficient reason for requiring the abandonment of projects there. Certainly there are no grounds for claiming complicity in human rights violations in a business project of this kind, since energy is used as much to promote human well being as to keep South Africa operating. Unless some further arguments can be offered about the riskiness of the investment itself, Westinghouse is not morally required to limit its investments in this case.

The arguments against corporations continuing business operations in South Africa are weak and seem to reflect more of an anti-corporation bias than they do fair and impartial analysis of moral issues. Moreover, the lack of concern shown by the church groups for the welfare of the corporation leads one to suspect that these groups are committed to the ideological assumption that corporations foster racism wherever they exist. Nevertheless, apartheid is clearly immoral, and corporations should show some awareness of this fact, as I believe many of them have. Furthermore, it is worth considering whether advocacy of *more* capitalism (freer and more private control of the economy) might not do more to correct racial tensions than proxy proposals that simply demand divestiture.

# V. Plant Closings

In early 1982 CBS's *60 Minutes* did a story on the closing of a GE plant in Ontario, California. Similar stories have been done by ABC and NBC as well. Indeed, plant closings often make national news, and some cities (e.g., Youngstown) are often identified in terms of the seemingly endless number of plant closings. The loss of jobs can be, and is, traumatic. Moreover, social problems, such as an increase in illness and crime, are often attributed to the closing of plants. Because of these problems at least 21 states have proposed legislation that would, to various degrees, restrict a firm's ability to close its plants. We must, therefore, examine both specific proposals directed at specific corporations and, also, make a few general remarks about plant closing legislation.

## A. *Proxy Resolutions on Plant Closings*

Besides proxy resolutions directed at companies doing business in South Africa, the Interfaith Center's publication contains a diverse set of other proposals devoted to the activities of private businesses. One such group of proposals centers around the issue of plant closings. Among the companies being petitioned by church groups on this issue are General Electric, Allis-Chalmers, Caterpillar Tractor, and U.S. Steel. In some cases (e.g., GE)[1] the resolution is less concerned with the question of plant closings than it is with whether the company will recognize unions in its new location. In other cases (e.g., U.S. Steel)[2] the resolution is largely a request for information about company policy on this issue. Our focus will be on those resolutions that make specific recommendations on what a company should do with respect to closing plants.

The following represents the proxy resolution submitted to Caterpillar Tractor Co. and is typical of many such resolutions:

> Be it therefore resolved that the shareholders request the Board of Directors to adopt a written policy for permanent or indefinite plant closings and mass layoffs, affecting 100 employees or more, which would include: 1. Committing Caterpillar to provide financial, technical and other assistance in retraining workers who are being laid off permanently or indefinitely so that they may qualify for current and future job openings; 2. Providing workers with information about current and expected job openings in their region as well as vocational counseling; 3. Providing advance public notice of at least six months of a plant closing and at least four months of a mass layoff; 4. giving dislocated workers first priority for jobs in other plants; 5. placing new installations in or near plants which are closing or losing operations.[3]

The first thing one notices about this resolution (and others like it) is its crudely utilitarian and redistributive character. Somehow the morality of the issue is supposed to be affected by the amount of people laid off. If there is a "mass" layoff or more than 100 employees are affected, the company should be concerned. Smaller amounts of layoffs are either of no concern or of substantially less serious concern. This utilitarian attitude is a thin disguise for the real issue here—redistribution. Since the kinds of companies that have 100 employees to lay off are also "big" companies, they can presumably afford to divert resources away from the business and towards "social" goals. Obviously, the net effect here is to benefit some people at the expense of the corporation.

The preceding remarks suggest that the Caterpillar resolution is another example of a proposal that violates the principle of responsible recommendation. It is clear that the church group which made this proposal has little or no interest in the financial viability or improvement of the corporation. The fifth proposal of the resolution is a clear indication of this. To require the company to put new installations in an area where other plants are closing or losing money is to ask the corporation to voluntarily submit itself to the same forces that destroyed other companies. Surely, no one concerned for the well-being of the corporation could make such a recommendation. Secondly, the issue of plant closings does not normally involve our first principle. Since employees do not have a right to their jobs (beyond whatever was contractually agreed to), no one's rights are violated if the plant closes, nor are anyone's rights violated if the five recommendations made by the church group are not followed.

It seems, then, that our third principle would be the one that might lead to the kinds of concerns expressed by the church proxy resolution. A corporation with a humane and open attitude about the effects of unemployment would surely take some steps to ease the transition. It is one thing, however, for a corporation to consider ways of easing a transition given its circumstances and quite another for it to have to live up to these five proposals. For example, it is quite likely to be the case that following these five recommendations would make some (very visible) people better off while at the same time hurting those who may have gotten the new jobs or the communities that may benefit in other ways by the existence of a new plant. The fourth principle of this proxy resolution is an explicit request to ignore the interests of those who might benefit from a change in plant location. Quite often plants are relocated in areas that have not enjoyed the economic benefits that have long been a part of the areas that originally had the plants. These are the (not very visible) people who suffer at the hands of groups who would restrict a corporation's freedom to relocate its plants. Indeed, the group that proposed this resolution gives no indication of any concern for those who will bear the cost of following these five principles.[4] Thus, given the narrow focus of who will benefit by implementing these five proposals, these church groups are at least as guilty as any corporation of violating our third principle.

The remaining three principles (1, 2, 3) of the resolution are also subject to at least one of the arguments given above. Nevertheless, it is worth briefly examining each. Apart from the expense involved, the first principle is ridiculous on the face of it. It asks the company to train workers for new jobs. This effectively means that the company must develop a side business of job training education; for if Caterpillar now makes tractors, and the jobs available are in computer programming, Caterpillar must educate workers in areas outside its competence. Furthermore, the closer the job description is to what the workers are already doing, the less persuasive is the case for job training, since they would already be fully or partially trained for similar jobs. Of course, the first principle *could* be saying that existing workers be given preference in training programs that would take place anyway for those who would fill new jobs in a new location. If this latter interpretation is applicable, it could make sense both financially and morally.

Companies often prefer workers they are familiar with (and who are familiar with the company) to new workers they do not know. Often these former employees are easier and less expensive to train. Moreover, companies that show little or no concern for their employees have morale problems and are not regarded as "good places to work." Thus, under these conditions retraining may provide a happy mixture of morality and sound business practice.

The second principle of the resolution concerns providing information to workers about job alternatives in the region. Depending on the costs of gathering this information, this second principle seems generally reasonable. The third principle (providing advanced notice of a closure or layoff) is a judgment call. On the surface giving advanced notice seems a reasonable and costless approach. However, advanced notices are sometimes followed by increased absenteeism because employees are out looking for new jobs or have left the firm. When this happens prior announcements can become very costly, and management has every incentive to keep the closing date secret. A much better alternative would be to negotiate severance pay and advanced notices of closings in the employee contracts in the first place.[5] It is important to realize, however, that any negotiations for severance pay and advanced notices of plant closings may involve trade-offs that some workers would be unwilling to make. In other words, workers may have to give something up in wages and/or fringe benefits to gain concessions in the areas of severance pay and advanced notification. It is improbable that all workers would evaluate equally the benefits of these trade-offs.

### B. *Plant Closing Legislation*

The purpose of the last section was not to recommend a lack of company concern over the impact on workers of plant closings, nor was it to say that workers would be foolish to trade wages and/or fringes for more security in the face of plant closings. The point was, rather, to indicate that, apart from any questions of individual rights, it is difficult or impossible to make any universal judgments about the "rights and wrongs" of plant closings. Nevertheless, it is interesting to note that within the Interfaith Center's publication almost all the proxy proposals look alike. This similarity among proxy proposals suggests a type of thinking that often leads to demands for legislation. Legislation is often recommended because it is thought that a uniform set of regulations can reasonably apply across a given political jurisdiction. The remarks that follow should indicate that matters are not so easily subject to generalizations, especially when they are backed by the power of the state.

Economist Richard B. McKenzie has studied the legislation on plant closings and has concluded that such legislation will worsen our economic problems rather than alleviate them.[6] The following represents a brief description of some of the conclusions McKenzie has drawn:

1. Since most plant closing laws exempt bankrupt firms, there are incentives for firms to arrange their financial affairs in order to declare bankruptcy when they announce their intentions to close.
2. Plant closing restrictions also end up being plant *opening* restrictions. Firms which may have once considered moving to a state will think twice when faced with restrictions on plant closings.
3. Plant closing legislation would be extremely costly. Had Firestone been subject to the closing restrictions of a current Ohio bill when it closed it's Dayton plant, it would have cost Firestone $60 million.
4. Closing restrictions can actually speed up closings. Since many firms are, at any given time, on the brink of closure, meeting the requirements for announcing a closing may have an adverse impact on the company and make it impossible to ride out tough economic periods.
5. Workers and consumers will end up bearing most of the costs of such legislation. Since the legislation will be costly, consumers will pay more for the same goods. Workers will face a declining number of new opportunities because fewer firms open plants in their states, and/or they will have to make concessions in wages and fringes to get the severance pay most bills now envision.
6. The human costs in terms of higher prices, lost economic opportunities, and declining tax revenues should not be ignored when the trauma of plant closings is discussed.

One can see from these few conclusions that there are many hidden costs to plant closing legislation. Indeed, the kind of short term thinking that goes into plant closing legislation does not square with the long run vantage point required by moral analysis.

We have not yet mentioned that plant closing legislation violates the rights of the owners by forcibly interfering with their freedom to use their property as they see fit. I do not wish to dwell on this point here because of its negative tone. Instead, let us put the point more positively. The solution to the plant closing problem is to take individual rights more seriously than governments now take them. Instead of responding to a problem by restricting behavior, governments should help to create a climate conducive to business investment. One example would be less oppressive taxation. Since "Proposition 2½" cut state taxes, manufacturing employment has risen in Massachusetts, and that state has one of the lowest unemployment rates. Moreover, less regulation and more sophistication in designing employment contracts to cover the contingencies of plant closings would also help.

It was once thought that the market system was a failure because labor and capital were not as mobile as market theory predicted. It is ironic that instead of encouraging further mobility, today's church groups (and others) are demanding more and more restrictions. Mobility does mean that some will be adversely affected by changing economic conditions. Restrictions on mobility, however, are likely to change the issue from one of plant closings to *firm* closings. The human costs that result from continued impediments to economic health are surely worth consideration by those who claim to have a "social conscience."

# VI. Employment Practices

## A. *Racial and Sexual Discrimination*

Another category of proxy resolutions involving employees deals with the area of employment practices, specifically to such issues as minority hiring, promotion of minority businesses, and equal pay for comparable work. A number of large companies have been the subject of these resolutions, including Westinghouse Electric, IT&T, AT&T, Sears, and Dart & Kraft.[1] Some of the resolutions (e.g., Dart & Kraft) are not particularly controversial, since they call for a new expression of commitment to past policies that may be affected by recent company reorganization. In general, however, Title VII of the 1964 Civil Rights act, as well as other regulations, do not leave companies much room for choice with respect to hiring. Thus, we shall focus on those matters not specifically required by law.

Three of the companies mentioned above (IT&T, AT&T, and Sears) have received almost identical proxy resolutions. Although the resolutions only call for a report, it is reasonable to assume that the areas to be reported upon are areas in which the petitioning group would demand action. The following is the relevant section of the Sears resolution calling for an explanation of company policy on:

> a. Present efforts to utilize and encourage minority enterprises providing various kinds of goods, services and construction by each department of the company's divisions; b. the percentage which minority business comprises of the company's overall business relationships; c. plans for future utilization and encouragement of minority businesses and plans to encourage reinvestment in minority communities.

The other two resolutions are virtually the same, except that the IT&T resolution included women as well as minorities.

Taken as recommendations for action, these three proposals are explicitly racist. No mention is made of, or concern shown for, the quality of the goods and services to be rendered by minority businesses or investments. Apparently, race alone is to be the decisive factor in making certain business decisions. It is not worthwhile to belabor this whole matter by analyzing the three proposals in terms of the general principles discussed in chapter three. It should be sufficient to note that these resolutions would have had a more plausible character to them if they had been simple affirmative action proposals. In other words, if the resolution had said something to the effect that given equal quality, price, and reliability a bias should exist in favor of minority businesses, the resolution might at least command respect. Incidently, it is worth noting that without a concern for quality, price, and reliability, any report issued by the company to the shareholders would convey no other information than statistical percentages. Even current law does not consider statistical percentages alone as decisive in determining discrimination or one's commitment to affirmative action.

Affirmative action is itself, however, of questionable moral value. This point can be made both in terms of the internal policy of the firm and in terms of society at large. With respect to the former, a firm's commitment to affirmative action will inevitably require some measurement of success with respect to that policy. This measurement will, in turn, most likely get expressed in quantitative terms (i.e., how many blacks, women, or other minorities do we need to have a successful affirmative action program). Once hiring of minorities or women is expressed in quantitative terms the firm is dangerously close to a quota system. Quotas are currently illegal and proponents of affirmative action prefer to speak in terms of "goals" rather than quotas. The difference is supposed to be that goals need only be pursued, but not necessarily met, whereas quotas are "hard and fast." Nevertheless, once "goals" are expressed in quantitative terms they do function in a manner that is similar to quotas even if not identical. If the "goal" is not met, the affirmative action program is almost invariably regarded as a failure, since all reasons given for not meeting the goal are interpreted as "not trying hard enough." If the "goal" is met suspicions are raised about it being treated as a minimum rather than a maximum target. Either way the employer is regarded as guilty until proven innocent and the employee often gets stamped as "less qualified." In fact, if affirmative action means anything other than staffing a position with the most qualified employee available, *it is virtually impossible ever to know for certain whether an employee hired under such a program was qualified or not*. And this uncertainty has the moral implication of depriving the employee of whatever respect that employee may deserve. Future performance may not correct this problem, and if it does it will take longer and promotions will themselves be seen only in terms of race or sex.

Other problems caused by affirmative action and/or preferential hiring include the problem of reverse discrimination. In *Weber v. Kaiser* (1979) the Supreme Court ruled that reverse discrimination to advance an affirmative action program was not a violation of Title VII. Companies were not required to use reverse discrimination, but if they did so they were not regarded by the court as violating the "spirit" of Title VII. This ruling raises some serious questions about whether it is justice or social engineering that the Court and government are now pursuing. If discrimination is wrong in one case, it is hard to imagine why discrimination would be right in another. The argument often given in defense of this policy of reverse discrimination is that it is rectification for past discrimination against the group now being favored. But this argument violates the moral principle that punishment should only be directed at those who actually cause or threaten harm, and the person excluded from an in-plant training program because he or she is not of the correct race or sex is unlikely to be the perpetrator of past harms. In any case, preferential hiring programs even further intensify the problem of being stamped as "less qualified" as discussed in the last paragraph.

The foregoing arguments, and others like them, are well known, but they often fail to be convincing. Part of the reason such arguments fail to persuade is that they seem too general and theoretical. Somehow everyone seems to know that in the real world corporations are discriminatory, and statistics are presented about particular corporations to prove discriminatory practices. Suppose, for example, that a corporation filled its entry level positions with over 80% women. Suppose also that only 60% of the promotions went to women. Isn't it obvious that such a corporation discriminates against women? Such statistical pictures are common and used to fuel the emotional fires that motivate charges of discrimination. Nevertheless, in a recent study by Professors Hoffman and Reed an actual "Fortune 500" company whose female labor force fit the statistical picture just described was studied.[2] It is worth noting some of the observations and conclusions of this study.

Hoffman and Reed subjected 850 of the corporation's employees to an exhaustive set of questions in double blind interviews (neither interviewers nor subjects knew the purpose of the questions). The researchers found that although the company promoted a slightly higher percentage of females requesting promotions than they did males, only 11% of the female clerks applied for promotion while 46% of the male clerks applied. Moreover, 25% of the males applying for promotion followed posted procedures for application whereas only 10% of the female employees did. The reasons for these discrepancies have more to do with socialization than they do with employer discrimination. Female employees tended to prefer pleasant working conditions to opportunities for promotion and saw their jobs as permanent rather than as a first step of a career.

Among the facts Hoffman and Reed uncovered about the differences between male and female attitudes are: 1) 8% of males and 26% of females indicated a lack of confidence in their ability to fill a supervisory position; 2) 12% of men and 28% of women said they would decline a promotion if it meant a transfer; 3) 4% of male clerks as opposed to 10% of female clerks said they expected to leave the labor force for a significant time before retirement; 4) a motivational index showed the males almost twice as motivated towards promotion than the females; and 5) marriage and children seemed to increase promotion seeking among males while decreasing it among females. Thus, the gross statistical discrepancies with which we began in no way indicate employer discrimination against their female work force. And similar conclusions, as we shall see below, indicate that this is not an isolated example. Hoffman and Reed conclude their study with a position that reflects the one taken here and is, thus, worth quoting in full.

> What is the company's obligation to its female employees? It is obliged to offer them the same opportunities as men, and to reward them in proportion to their productivity. No more. But it should be the requirement of companies to provide opportunity to all its members at all levels. It cannot, indeed *should* not, compensate women—or anyone else—for effort expended in the service of other commitments. Even if those external commitments fall more heavily on women, the inequalities (if such they are) of early socialization or of the division of labor in the household are not the responsibility nor the business, in any sense of that word, of an employer.

> If a company is so moved, however, it might reasonably seek to rationalize both its internal labor market and its relations to the external market—examining its seniority systems, lines of progression, training programs, and so forth. In these areas, employers may find that they can serve the interests of their employees from "protected groups" while serving their own as well, by expanding the range of opportunities for *individuals,* and rewarding those who seize them.

To indicate that the kinds of conclusions drawn by Hoffman and Reed were not isolated, we must conclude this section of the chapter by looking at discrimination on a broader social scale. The usual way social critics do this is to look at aggregate statistical percentages, notice a differential in pay and promotions between white males and minorities or women, and then conclude that this difference is based upon discrimination. The assumption underlying this approach is that in the absence of discrimination no ethnic group would differ substantially from any other. This approach has been criticized by numerous authors on both theoretical and statistical grounds. For the sake of brevity, let us list some of the conclusions drawn by two economists—Thomas Sowell and Walter Williams.[3] The following represent the non-discriminatory factors that contribute to income differentials and which substantially narrow or eliminate the statistical gap between white males and other groups customarily attributed to discrimination.

1. *Age:* There is an average age differential of 10 to 20 years between ethnic groups at opposite ends of income distribution. The younger the worker, the less likely he or she is to command higher salaries.
2. *Education:* The lowest income groups have only recently begun to finish high school and attend college. Obviously, the less education one has, the less likely it will be that one gets a larger salary.
3. *Geography:* Income differentials are greater between states (e.g., California and Mississippi) than between whites and blacks. Blacks in one state may earn half of those in another, and aggregate statistics do not reflect this.
4. *Historical Differences:* Different ethnic groups place different value upon the work ethic and choice of occupations. This tends to over-represent some ethnic groups in some industries while under-representing them in others (e.g., Germans in beer production).
5. *Marriage:* Single women in their thirties who have worked continuously since high school actually earn higher salaries than their white male counterparts. Married women often interrupt their careers and then re-

enter the labor force. Obviously, being absent from the labor force for some time will tend to diminish one's salary. Moreover, some ethnic groups (e.g., Mexican Americans) tend to marry earlier than others (e.g., the Japanese). This affects educational opportunities and consistent employment which in turn affects wages.

6. *Barriers to entry:* Many laws or regulations, such as Davis-Bacon, the National Labor Relations Act, minimum wage, and occupational licensing discourage or prevent minorities and women from competing for contracts and jobs. Thus, these groups tend to be under-represented in certain areas quite apart from discrimination.

These criteria suggest that income differentials can be attributed to factors other than racial or sexual discrimination—a point that confirms on a social level what Hoffman and Reed found at a "micro" level. When aggregate statistical differentials are not analyzed in terms of these criteria, false inferences are drawn. Moreover, the kind of reasoning that ignores these criteria can create anomalies. For example, Professor Williams has discovered that black female professionals actually do 25% better than their white female counterparts! Surely, one would not want to conclude that white females were discriminated against in favor of black females.

My argument is not that there is no discrimination in the business world, although the amount there is may be statistically undetectable when the factors listed above are considered. Rather my argument is that 1) no corporation is obligated to pursue a course of affirmative action if justification for that course of action is based on simplistic thinking about income differentials and ignores considerations of cost and quality, and 2) corporations are not obligated to participate in what amounts to redistributive schemes or schemes to re-socialize groups along lines considered desirable by representatives of certain ideologies. Church groups which find cases where a company does not reward individuals according to their contributions to the firm have grounds for protest. Unfortunately, most of the proxy proposals found in the ICCR publication seem little concerned with this last point.

In all the shouting over affirmative action and preferential hiring, one moral consideration goes almost completely undiscussed—how the employer is treated. Employers have been forced to change employment criteria which have a disproportionate impact on minorities *even in the absence of discriminatory intent.*"[4] Moreover, the employer must submit affirmative action plans to government agencies at their whim whether or not there is any reason to believe discrimination is present. As Professor Sowell puts it:

> The employer whose numbers do not fit the preconceptions of government agencies, and who does not prove himself innocent to those same agencies, must then fashion a "remedy." The agencies involved do not specify what he is to do. They approve or disapprove plans he submits. In this way, they avoid the legal onus of themselves prescribing quotas in violation of the Civil Rights Act, while adding to the process costs of the employer, who must guess at what size quotas will satisfy them—and continue to resubmit plans until he guesses right.[5]

Simply preparing an affirmative action report can cost a company hundreds of thousands of dollars, *no matter what the end result of the process may be*! Here, certainly, is a concrete example of the social permission theorist's claim that businesses are nothing more than "trustees" of society's resources. Not only are employers treated in ways that anyone else would consider to be a violation of his civil rights (by having the burden of proof placed on him rather than the government), but they are also required to bear the expense of such schemes even if they are found innocent. This sort of social engineering violates all three of our principles simultaneously.

## B. *Equal Pay for Comparable Work*

The Westinghouse Electric proxy resolution contains some of the features of the resolutions just discussed, but it adds that the company must "ensure that all compensation incorporate the principle of equal pay for comparable work."[6] In this particular case, it is not clear whether the group which proposed the resolution understands its own proposal. The material surrounding the resolution itself ties the comparable work concept to racial discrimination. But the comparable work concept and racial discrimination are not conceptually related. The former refers to giving equal pay for different but comparable jobs. Race need not factor into the comparable work principle at all.

The concept of comparable work actually began in 1942 when the National War Labor Board issued General Order No. 16. This order called for pay adjustments which "equalize the wage or salary rates paid to females with the rates paid to males for comparable quality and quantity of work on the same or similar operations.'"[7] Since 1942 the EQUAL PAY ACT and Title VII of the CIVIL RIGHTS ACT have been used by comparable work advocates to justify their cause. However, Congress explicitly rejected comparable work in favor of the stricter "equal pay for equal work" with respect to the EQUAL PAY ACT. But there have been other legal rulings and state decisions that seem to support comparable work. In 1981, for example, California adopted a comparable work rule for state jobs. And in *Gunther vs. County of Washington* the court ruled in favor of female jail matrons who were being paid less than males doing similar work. It should be emphasized, on the other hand, that there is currently scanty legal support for comparable work beyond what has just been mentioned. The current Supreme Court, moreover, is moving cautiously if at all on this matter. We are, thus, in a position to assess the value of this concept *before* it has a chance of becoming the law of the land, rather than afterwards.

The first problem with comparable work is that it assumes that wages are determined by job descriptions in the personnel office's manual or that corporations *create* wages rather than *respond* to them. Except in the immediate short term, wages are determined by market conditions, so any call for comparable work rules is really a call for the elimination of market forces. Secondly, comparable work is a concept that is based upon a theory of value of extremely dubious credentials—namely, an intrinsic theory of value. Such a theory holds that the value of something is determined solely by the nature of the thing in question irrespective of who may value it and how much they are willing to give up to obtain it. Applied to jobs, the intrinsic theory would hold that jobs have an intrinsic value which can somehow be intuited and assigned a monetary value. Needless to say, no job has such a value, and the attempt to intuit the value leads to the final problem—how to make the comparisons. Is janitorial work comparable to yard maintenance? Are skilled electricians comparable to middle managers? What possible basis could there be for answering such questions apart from arbitrary fiat? Moreover, there seems to be no limit to the criteria that can be used to make the comparisons. For example, are medical doctors comparable to janitors? On the basis of the education required to do the job they are not comparable. But if our basis was years of service to the firm, or having a pleasant personality, or providing a comfortable environment for customers, they might be comparable.

The rationale for the concept of comparable work is discrimination, and the same types of aggregate income differentials noted above are cited to justify legal and moral action. However, the comparable work concept is significantly more sinister than either affirmative action or preferential hiring. The difference is that affirmative action and/or preferential hiring seek to "correct" certain outcomes of market processes or rectify past injustices. Comparable work, on the other hand, implies the *replacement* of the market system. Instead of employers paying salaries or wages based on market conditions and market price, salaries and wages will be determined in terms of some other job being used as a standard of comparison. Even if the job that is being used as a standard of comparison is itself priced by the market, it could itself be compared to some third job category which would render the market price of the former job meaningless. Furthermore, if a job were being used as a standard of comparison for a *number* of other jobs, this would tend to remove it from the marketplace, since the market price for any job is always a function of how it compares to other alternative jobs and how much those now doing the job are able to bargain for from employers. The more jobs compared to the job serving as the standard of comparison by other than market means, the less meaningful is the market price of the job being used as the standard of comparison.

Simply put, once some means other than the pricing system of the market is used to compare jobs, the distortions in the market will have to be corrected *simply to discover the real value of the job being used as the standard of comparison.*[8] There are only two ways to go in making these corrections: 1) return to a market pricing system, or 2) interfere further with the market. The first alternative would mean abandoning the comparable work concept, so it is likely that the same groups which originally pushed for comparable work would call for continued interference until market pricing would be altogether abandoned. Obviously we are a long way away from abandoning the market pricing system as a means for determining wages. However, once a governmentally backed program gets rolling, its direction is almost never reversed.

Comparble work as social policy is subversive of the market, in violation of individual rights and freedoms, arbitrary, and suggestive of a centrally planned economy. Nevertheless, such clear cut conclusions are sometimes more difficult to draw in specific cases. Assuming a commitment to profits, quality, and our third rule of moral openness, a firm may discover some discrepancies in pay that may warrant attention.

Employee morale, fairness, and the ability to attract ever better personnel are advantageous to both employer and employee. Such considerations may make it desirable for employers to correct certain pay differentials *on a very limited and specific basis,* whether that correction is made between the same job or very similar ones. Discrimination is morally improper because a) it treats people not as individuals but as members of a collective, and b) because it shifts the focus away from what is relevant (job performance) to what is irrelevant (race or sex). Thus, an employer sensitive to human relations issues will not want to be perceived as having policies that look discriminatory. And it has never been my point in this chapter to argue that no realistic cases of discrimination can be found in the business world. The church groups (and others) do not, however, petition corporations from the limited standpoint just mentioned. It is either ignorance or hatred of the market that moves these groups. Their zeal for their cause might do an injustice not only to employers, but also help encourage the kind of simplistic thinking that eventually *increases* social strife and conflict.

# VII. Pollution and Environmental Protection

> To our way of thinking, it's not progress when you create sickness, maim our countryside and irreplaceable wilderness areas, needlessly kill animals and endanger human beings, just so some misguided industrialists can show an ever-growing record profit.
>
> David R. Brower, President, *Friends of the Earth*

> There is little question that man can destroy himself and mutilate the earth's ecosystem; but if he does, it is more likely to be the result of political and social folly than because of industrial pollution.
>
> Cy A. Adler, author, *Ecological Fantasies*

Despite the generally negative assessment of the proxy resolutions examined in the preceding chapters, not all the resolutions one finds in the ICCR publication necessarily deserve rejection. Some of the resolutions, if founded on fact, concern matters that may fall under the category of rights violations. For example, both Upjohn and Occidental Petroleum have been accused of emitting toxic substances into the air and drinking water respectively.[1] The Upjohn resolution demands a specific course of action to correct the problem, while the Occidental resolution calls for an environmental impact report. The charges against Occidental are, however, more serious than those against Upjohn, since there is some ambiguity about the exact nature of the safety hazard involved in the Upjohn case.[2] Consider, then, this example from the supporting statement to the Occidental resolution:

> Internal Hooker memoranda indicate that spills of highly toxic PCB's, leaking drums of toxic chemicals and the risk of leaching of dangerous pollutants into groundwater supplies, were all associated with Hooker's Hicksville, Long Island, N.Y. plant. Company sources also document that in Lathrop, California, Occidental knowingly and illegally polluted local drinking water supplies and then hid this information from local authorities. Furthermore, SEC proceedings indicate

> that Occidental knowingly supplied false information to the EPA. We feel that, in addition to federal and local authorities, Occidental has hidden mismanagement of toxic waste disposal from its own stockholders.

If any of these charges are true, some action to correct the problem must, indeed, be taken. Moreover, it may also be the case that management acted in a morally illegitimate fashion when it considered alternative courses of action in the past.

### A. *Theoretical Approaches to Pollution*

Although it is clear that activities which threaten life and health are not permissible, it is not so obvious how to correct the problem. Since air and water are public goods, the system as it now stands gives every incentive for a company to increase it's profits by externalizing the costs to others. In other words, if I can dump my garbage in the public domain, I have saved the cost of having to process it myself and have transferred that cost to others. One solution might be to take the proxy resolution approach and hope that management has a conscience or that stockholder pressure will force proper behavior. However, stockholders have roughly the same incentives as management to transfer costs.

The moral problem associated with pollution can be stated simply enough: one person cannot dump his garbage on another person's property without the latter's permission. The solution to this problem is either to get permission or to find some other way to harmlessly process one's waste. There is, of course, a third alternative—one that seems to be at the core of the positions of many extremist environmental groups. The third position is that producing garbage is wrong, and thus the problem can be solved by stopping the production of garbage. Notice that this third position is categorical in form while the first two seek alternatives or allow for accommodation. If the first two solutions are combined into a single (oversimplified) prototype, it is not pollution per se that is condemned but, rather, the condition in which people are imposed upon against their will. This can be contrasted with the "pollution-is-bad" mentality where it is pollution itself that is being condemned.

If we want to think clearly about the pollution problem, it is important that we avoid the "pollution-is-bad" mentality. Since pollution is the by-product of any production process, including breathing, the "pollution-is-bad" mentality can only lead to dogmatic moralizing and hysteria and, perhaps, to the destruction of economic progress and technology. We need to rethink what pollution is so that we can move towards the moral goal of removing the conflict of obligations between not harming the public and maximizing profits. The first step in realizing this goal is to understand that *everyone wants pollution,* although the amounts and degrees may vary. A more positive way of putting the same point is to say that people want environmental purity *as one good among many others.* Given a choice, few (if any) would trade the benefits of technology for complete environmental purity, just as few (if any) would completely sacrifice the environment for the most marginal of technological benefits. It would be morally (and practically) ideal, therefore, if individuals could communicate to each other the values they place upon various alternative goods.

Traditionally, the way to allow for individual choice with respect to goods and services is to: a) regard people as having entitlements to various goods and services, and b) allow freedom of trade in the things people are entitled to, thus creating a market in those goods and services. There is no reason in principle why a good like environmental purity should be treated differently from other goods. Polluters would have to either get permission from those who would be affected by their pollution or they would have to reduce their pollution levels to the point where they could secure such permission. By the same token, consumers would have to allocate their own resources so that the value each person places on environmental quality could be compared to other values and expressed in the "marketplace." Through trade individuals would have an increasing number of options offering the right mix of environmental quality and other goods. Although polluters would have to initially expend more resources to solve the pollution problem (since they initiated the action), eventually an optimal mix of alternative goods would result.

The foregoing may seem to some to be utopian. There are, indeed, some practical problems associated with the plan, such as establishing entitlements (property rights) in such mediums as air and water. But the basic principles are sound and have even been recommended in limited form by the EPA itself![3] The preceding discussion indicates, contrary to the reasoning of many "environmentalists," that the pollution problem results from *common* property rather than private property. As economist Dwight Lee puts the issue:

> With privately owned resources, people have the information and motivation to employ more of each resource only so long as the value it provides to them is at least as great as the value it would otherwise provide to others. With commonly owned receptor resources, people are motivated to employ these resources as waste-sinks as long as the value to them of doing so is positive, regardless of the value that others forego as a consequence. From the perspective of the efficient allocation of our resources, our receptor resources are over-used as waste-sinks relative to their use for providing environmental quality.[4]

Lee and others, therefore, recommend that the principles of private ownership and market exchange be applied to the pollution problem.

The usual solution is to call for more governmental management of resources and stricter regulation. This approach does not get to the heart of the matter, since it still leaves the resources in the public domain and subject to the same kind of incentives to transfer costs (although from and to different groups). Moreover, there are serious questions about how well this approach has been working.[5] The other, and more promising alternative, is to use the property rights approach to solve environmental problems. The property rights approach would be consistent with the kind of moral theory advanced here, but the whole question is too complex for present discussion. In general the proponents of this alternative to government control either propose that pollution be treated as a tort and/or that property rights be created in air and water.[6] The point of using the property rights approach is to solve the problem at the root by internalizing the costs of pollution. If we can more closely approximate a situation where those who reap the benefits of their production also are responsible for the costs, individual freedom of choice will be encouraged and no one will have to subsidize the values of others. Market structures using private property rights accomplish this goal better than the collectivized solutions of government. The next two sections should demonstrate that this last claim is not simply over-generalized abstract theory.

### B. *The Non-Solution of Government Control*

The pollution issue provides the opportunity for us to observe a growing, and disturbing, tendency among not just church groups but the public in general. Faced with a social problem the current tendency is to call for more government regulation. Ignoring for the moment those who seek more government control as a matter of ideological principle, the call for government to solve social problems is fraught with innumerable and insurmountable difficulties. Even though many people believe that government regulation is a speedy, cheap, and simple process, the exact opposite is more often than not true. John T. Dunlop has summarized some of these problems,[7] and I shall list them here:

1. Government regulation promotes simplistic thinking about issues. Each side of an issue exaggerates its story to get favorable legislation passed.
2. Designing and administering programs is very complicated and, thus, costly and slow.
3. Policies which appear straightforward often have the opposite effect of the intent of the regulation.
4. Rule-making and adjudicating tends to be slow which causes costly delays and conflicts among groups petitioning for exemptions.
5. There is no mechanism for creating mutual accommodation among conflicting interest groups. Thus, there is no way to discover anyone's true position.
6. Regulatory efforts are rarely abandoned once they are put in force, no matter how out-dated.
7. There is a great deal of legal game playing. Regulators and regulatees battle constantly in court, undermining the implementation of the program.
8. Regulations are most often designed for large companies but are applied uniformly to small and medium sized firms to whom they may not be applicable.
9. Once the regulatory function of an agency is established, the work becomes routine and is, thus, attractive to only the mediocre.
10. Uniform regulations are often inherently unworkable, since society itself is not uniform.
11. There is often a great deal of regulatory overlap with different agencies sharing similar functions and jealously guarding their turf. This causes waste, confusion, and uncoordinated activity.

The general problems listed above increase costs, create delays, and often produce counter-productive results. Moreover, these same problems are not restricted to traditional areas of manufacturing. They crop up in the environmental area as well. Indeed, the types of problems just mentioned seem to be an *essential* part of the way government handles social problems and not merely an accidental or occasional problem.

To lend support to the idea that governmentally controlled solutions do not yield the best results and that this is due to the nature of government itself, economist Peter Aranson has described four main areas of governmental problems in environmental regulation:[8]

1. The General Problem of Political Failure
2. Interest Group Intervention
3. Congressional Incentives
4. Bureaucratic Incentives

With respect to the first category, Aranson asks us to imagine that we have in fact discovered an optimal public policy of environmental quality that has not yet been enacted or implemented by an administrative agency.[9] Since it is obvious that no matter what policy one wants some people will oppose it, lobbying efforts must be undertaken to convince those in power and fend off attacks from opposing groups. But this is expensive—more expensive than any *particular* individual is likely to wish to pay for. Moreover, the benefits of the adoption of the public policy will be received by everyone even if they do not help in its adoption. Thus, since incentives for support are weak because of the expense and because one may get the benefits without participating, the optimal policy will either be difficult to implement or unlikely to take optimal form if it is implemented. Aranson sums up this way:

> Political action leading to the enactment, implementation, enforcement, and judicial protection of an optimal public policy toward environmental quality is identical to private action to supply a public good, such as a cleaner lake. It faces the same problems. Manifestly, therefore, if we expect to find market failure then we should also expect to find political failure, and for precisely the same reasons.[10]

Interest group intervention poses another problem for governmental control, and this problem arises out of the first. Since policies acceptable to the public at large face the problems just mentioned, interest groups form to meet the expenses mentioned above. These groups, however, push their own *particular* programs. Satisfaction of the values of the interest group is the goal—not necessarily (or even probably) the interests of all those likely to be affected by any policy. For example,

30% of all environmental groups have virtually no members at all! Furthermore, the larger environmental groups provide income, prestige, and visibility for the "public interest" lawyers that carry forth their causes. As Aranson puts it:

> For its leaders and employees, an environmental-interest group is equivalent to a firm that provides distinctly private, divisible benefits. The necessity to sustain the flow of such benefits, not the larger public interest, colors the group's actions, especially with respect to the bureau with which it interacts.[11]

In addition, manufacturers of antipollution devices can exert influence as well. Most economists agree that performance based standards (which set maximum allowable limits to discharges) are preferable to design-based standards which dictate the particular technology to be used. Performance based standards allow flexibility in the choice of equipment to meet requirements and can encourage competition among suppliers of such technologies. Nevertheless, the EPA has shown a strong penchant for design based technologies which may, in part, be attributable to the influence of producers of antipollution equipment. Finally, governments and representatives from various states and regions can constitute an interest group in the environmental area. Evidence for this will be provided in the next section.

Congress itself faces incentives to pass inefficient policies on environmental quality. Aranson describes two major types of such incentives. The first is the propensity among congressmen to give preference to the views of upper and upper-middle class constituents. Not only are such groups better organized and better able to afford to articulate their values than are the lower classes, but it is the upper classes of this country that make up the vast majority of the members of environmental groups.[12] Secondly, congressmen need to pass concrete goods along to their constituents and/or be easily identified with specific pieces of legislation. Since the chances are small for a single congressman's name to be associated with a major piece of national legislation, a congressman can usually make his mark by getting specific projects for his district or state (e.g., a special water pollution project) and/or getting exemptions for certain constituents from legislation or regulations already in force. Oddly enough, the more unreasonable the legislation the better it is for congressmen. Passing such legislation helps to silence vocal interest groups while at the same time providing numerous opportunities for getting special exemptions for constituents or for passing amendments to which a congressman's name can be easily associated.

Finally, we come to the area of bureaucratic incentives. The classical view of government bureaucracy is that an organization such as the EPA is a neutral body implementing and enforcing the wishes of the people as expressed through their congressmen. Few people today are so naive as to believe in the classical view. A more realistic model is that bureaucrats and their agencies act in their own self-interest. In this connection, Aranson lists four operational rules of bureaucracy that help explain what the incentives are. These rules have little to do with what will benefit the public at large:

1. maximizing the agency's budget
2. expanding the agency's jurisdiction
3. maximizing its monitorable output
4. minimizing detectable errors

During the years of 1971 to 1980 the EPA's budget increased at an average of 44% per year. This includes one year where the budget increased 264%, although it also includes two years of negative budget growth. These increases substantially expanded the staff and the capacity for regulatory interference by the EPA, especially in areas where the EPA does not belong, such as setting design based technological standards. Secondly, the EPA has succeeded in expanding its jurisdiction by using three different strategies: a) careful interaction with congressmen, b) utilization of interest groups, and c) differential regulatory standards. With respect to the first, Aranson notes the following:

> The EPA's leaders have understood that the members of Congress are concerned with dispensing private, divisible benefits to their constituents. Accordingly, the EPA's water projects, which are really public-works projects, constitute the bulk of its funding. These projects are traditional, old-fashioned, garden variety, pork-barrel programs, identical to such standbys as the River and Harbor Bill. These projects give the EPA a tremendous base of local support, which is reflected in the Congress.[13]

The EPA has also given grants and advice on preparing testimony to various interest groups. These groups are often used on a state level to enhance the EPA's influence over areas the Federal government had left to the states. Furthermore, the EPA has been conservative in regulating existing pollution but extremely strict with new sources. As Aranson notes, "This strategy tends to preserve the agency's jurisdiction while muting criticism of its incessant imperialism."[14]

The third rule of bureaucratic operation concerns maximizing monitorable output. Since it is difficult for a bureau such as the EPA to tell whether its policies are successful, the tendency is to redefine success in terms of activity and then seek to maximize activity. First of all, the EPA "will seek out as many varieties and sources of pollution as possible and will exaggerate their dangers to the maximum extent possible, short of damaging credibility."[15] Secondly, the EPA (and any other agency) will tend to define its success in the *number* of regulatory rules it can implement. Finally, the EPA will be reluctant to do retroactive studies on the effects of its rules. And when such studies are done, the results predictably favor the EPA in the sense that the studies show an "alarming" lack of compliance with EPA rules.

The final major incentive bureaucrats have is to minimize detectable errors. In the case of the EPA this amounts to regulating pollution at zero risk. The EPA is currently empowered to regulate pollution that would harm the most susceptible persons of any population. This same zero risk strategy is being contemplated for the implementation of the Toxic Substances Control Act. Aranson notes the problems with this approach.

> A policy goal of creating zero levels of environmental risk merely shifts risk to other margins, such as business and economic failure and the attendant but unrecorded and undetectable health losses that accompany such calamities. The EPA now reports to the Department of Labor the loss of jobs in the United States caused by the implementation of its regulations. This accounting is inadequate, because it records only the destruction of pre-existing jobs. It does not calculate the number of potential jobs that never materialize because of EPA activities, nor does it measure the number of jobs that materialize in foreign countries with less-strict environmental standards.[16]

### C. *A Case In Point: The Clean Air Act*

The perverse governmental incentives discussed above can be examined concretely with respect to the Clean Air Act of 1970 and its amendments of 1977. Although detailed discussion is beyond the scope of this chapter, I can highlight some of the problems connected with the Clean Air Act that demonstrate some of the points I have just made. Let me begin with the role self-interest has played in a piece of legislation that is supposed to be in the interest of the general public.

From an important study by B. Peter Pashigian we learn that regional self-interest had more to do with the Clean Air Act than did a dispassionate concern for the welfare of all.[17] In his study Pashigian argues that environmental legislation has more to do with attenuating the competition among regions and between rural and urban interests than it does with public health or fair treatment. Northeastern urban areas have effectively lobbied for environmental benefits to themselves at the expense of others and have used environmental legislation as a vehicle for preventing the movement of industry to the sun belt or other less developed areas. As Pashigian puts it: "The political strength of urban residents in developed states permitted an improvement of environmental conditions via federal policy without imposing the full costs of the improvement on urban residents."[18]

Regional biases can perhaps be best observed in the fight over the "no significant deterioration" (NSD) amendments to the Clean Air Act. NSD essentially requires that plants locating in new areas cannot significantly deteriorate the surrounding environment. In effect this means that areas of a state or regions of the country that are less developed and have "higher quality" air will be seriously handicapped in attracting new businesses. What the Pashigian study shows is that coalitions of Northeastern urban Democrats blocked any attempts by less developed states to weaken NSD amendments. A similar result was obtained when Pashigian examined the voting records of urban and rural interests *within* a state.

> In summary, the analysis of the votes on the Nondegredation Amendments suggests that urban areas supported the amendments in part to raise the cost of mobility to rural or less developed areas...Conversely, congressmen representing rural and less developed areas opposed the nondeterioration policy because these districts hoped to attract industry.[19]

The Clean Air Act was sold to the public as public interest legislation designed to protect public health. If this were true, then one would expect to find the highest pollution abatement costs in those places with the dirtiest air. "However, if political self-interest dominates national or public interest, we would expect to see the reverse cost pattern—higher pollution abatement costs per unit of output for plants located in the southern and western regions."[20] Professor Pashigian found that southern and western states had *higher* rather than lower pollution abatement costs. This is because stricter regulations were placed on new plants rather than existing plants—indicating once again that health considerations take second place to political maneuvering.

More recently Pashigian has done a study on how environmental regulations have affected small plants. As he points out:

> The results are disquieting, for they show, among other things, that environmental regulation has reduced the number of plants and raised average plant size in industries with major clean-up problems.[21]

Compliance with regulation is costly, and if one adds to that the more severe standards the EPA applies to new plants, the advantage clearly goes to large established plants. These results give one pause not only because of the economic effects, but also because the same groups which harp on the "evils of big corporations" and advocate environmental purity seem to be encouraging the very problems they seek to correct. Moreover, Pashigian's study shows that resources shift away from labor and towards capital because of environmental regulation. This too should give one pause in light of the concerns I noted in my chapter on plant closings. Pashigian's findings cause him to conclude in the following manner:

> Environmental rules have not only reduced the number of plants in the affected industries, but have made it more difficult for small plants to compete with large. While the study cannot definitely determine that environmental regulation has harmed *both* large and small plants, it does show that small plants have been harmed relative to large plants. It also shows that more funds are being allocated to capital compared to labor.[22]

Other authors have noted additional problems and costs resulting from the Clean Air Act (especially given the 1977 amendments). Kenneth W. Chilton and Ronald J. Penoyer mention the following: 1) the conflict between our clean air policy and our energy policy, 2) retardation of the development of synthetic fuels, and 3) delays caused by the need for permits.[23] If, for example, we look only at the third category, we find that companies must obtain EPA approval before they can proceed with their business activities. This means that until a company gets an official stamp of approval, they must hold up production. Moreover, it is expensive for companies to petition for such approval. In this regard, Professor Neil Orloff of the Cornell Law School has documented some of the problems with this system of obtaining permission:[24]

1. Of the 1,527 applications submitted to the Environmental Protection Agency in the last six years in regions that have attained national air-quality standards, 27 percent are still pending.
2. About 45 percent of the applications have been pending for more than a year, while the EPA has denied only a single permit.
3. It takes an average of three years to obtain a permit under the Clean Air Act, and often more than four years.
4. The average cost of submitting an application is $250,000 to $300,000—not including costs that might result from the risk of redesign, changed location, abandoned projects or court action.

In response to these problems, Orloff notes that, "the law needs to be restructured so that once a company complies with the standards it can proceed without waiting for a government official's stamp of approval."[25] The delays not only cost companies money, but perhaps export jobs to areas with less bureaucratic control. These are completely counter-productive costs, since they contribute nothing to the quality of the environment.

## D. *Conclusion*

My focus in the last two sections on the costs of government regulation was not designed to claim that there are absolutely no benefits resulting from environmental legislation. However, it was my intention to indicate that the same or additional benefits could be obtained by removing or restructuring governmentally controlled programs and regulations. Moreover, I sought to show some problems inherent in the very nature of governmental solutions to the environmental difficulties we face. It should be clear by this time that naive trust in federal legislation and regulation is misplaced. In general, then, one of our conclusions must be that moves towards decentralization would be a desirable first step. Furthermore, a system of specific and alienable property rights should be developed for resources currently in the public domain.

This would encourage people to more accurately assess the value they place on environmental quality. If a system of property rights cannot be developed in the near future, more market like approaches should be sought (e.g., performance instead of design based standards, saleable pollution rights, etc.). These market approaches at least more closely approximate what would be found in a system of pure individual rights than do governmentally imposed solutions.

This chapter began with an examination of proxy proposals directed at corporations involved with toxic wastes. As I noted at the beginning of the chapter, toxic wastes (almost by definition) pose a real health threat to almost any member of a proximate community. Thus, my principle of the protection of individual rights might concur with the church groups on this point. But it must also be remembered that less is known about the effects of toxic waste clean-ups and legislation than about air and water pollution. And given what we described earlier about the dangers of regulation, another blind move to rush into a federally controlled "solution" may end up with the same problems already documented. The legitimate moral concerns of the church groups in this area can only be constructive if they abandon their tendency towards collectivized approaches and come to see both the practical efficiency and moral superiority of market alternatives.

# VIII. Nuclear Technology

God did not make plutonium, and therefore it is evil.

(Creative Initiative Foundation)

The "division" among scientists on nuclear power, then, is a peculiar one. To put it brutally, but fairly accurately, it is a division between those who know what they are talking about and those who don't.

Dr. Petr Beckman, Author, *The Health Hazards of Not Going Nuclear*

## A. *Nuclear Power Production*

By far the largest number of proxy resolutions contained in the Interfaith Center's publication concerns nuclear technology. The combined resolutions account for over 20% of all the proxy resolutions contained in the Interfaith Center's publication.[1] Quasi-public firms such as utilities enter into this picture on two fronts: 1) nuclear reactors, and 2) the reprocessing of nuclear waste for nuclear weapons. The remaining proxy resolutions are directed at companies in the private sector who make nuclear weapons. The nuclear issue can be divided into concern over U.S. arms policy and concern over the safety of generating nuclear power.

A fair assessment of the nuclear power issue indicates that the safety of these plants has not been unambiguously determined.[2] Moreover, I am not qualified to evaluate the technical questions surrounding nuclear safety. Both these statements seem to be required by our principles of responsible recommendation and moral consideration. These principles do not, however, seem to be shared by the ideological church groups submitting proxy resolutions. For some reason, they do not seem to worry about their own qualifications when they call a specific form of energy conversion "unsafe." For example, consider the following supporting statement to a proxy resolution submitted to Union Electric Company:[3]

> Nuclear power can no longer be considered safe, cheap and clean. It has many inherent dangers, is increasingly expensive and nuclear wastes cause a real health hazard for the human community of today and of the future. We believe that...the Callaway nuclear plant will be detrimental to the quality of human life and destructive of our good earth.

It is not, of course, the right to make such statements that is in question, here. Rather, the foregoing statement indicates the incredible lack of modesty the authors of the proposal show in presenting "facts" about a rather technical issue. Furthermore, this statement indicates an equally disturbing propensity to over generalize ("destructive of our good earth") and to use ambiguous or meaningless slogans ("quality of life").

Even though we are not in a position to evaluate the technical questions surrounding nuclear safety, we are in a position to present some points that are seldom mentioned by the media and which call into question the common assumption that nuclear power is unambiguously harmful, dangerous, or risky. If some significant arguments can be presented in support of nuclear power, it cannot be the case that there is any general obligation to refrain from pursuing nuclear power as an energy source or that a utility company is necessarily being socially irresponsible if it continues to produce nuclear power. This can be said even if we are not in a position to evaluate the technical side of the question, since claiming a general obligation requires an unambiguous factual and moral footing—neither of which are to be found in this issue.

Consider first of all the question of whether nuclear power has the support of the scientific community. One way to measure this support is to list some of the professional scientific groups that support nuclear power.

1. The American Nuclear Society (after 21 years of refusing to commit themselves until they were certain of the superiority of nuclear power).
2. The Power Engineering Society (18,000 members)
3. The Energy Committee of the Institute of Electrical and Electronics Engineers (170,000).
4. The Society of Professional Engineers (69,000 members).

5. The National Council of the American Institute of Chemical Engineers (39,000 members).
6. The Board of Directors of the Health Physics Society (3,400 members).

In 1975 25,000 scientists and engineers signed a "Declaration of Energy Independence" in support of nuclear power (and coal) and submitted it to the White House. On the other hand, the Union of Concerned Scientists mailed an anti-nuclear petition to 15,000 scientists. Only 2,300 signed the petition which is a relatively small percentage of the groups targeted for mailing and only 0.3% of the scientists in the physical and life sciences.[4] Moreover, most of the scientists against nuclear power (including the prominent ones) are not themselves nuclear scientists or nuclear engineers. Even though the media gives its attention to vocal anti-nuclear scientists, there is no evidence whatsoever of general scientific support for the anti-nuclear power movement.

The lack of expert scientific support for the anti-nuclear movement has not gone unnoticed by opponents of nuclear power. The current ploy to overcome this problem is to argue that experts ought to disqualify themselves from the nuclear debate. Lorna Salzman of the Friends of the Earth puts it this way:

> No nuclear scientist with a connection to nuclear power profit making has a right to bludgeon government and citizens into accepting a death-dealing technology, a technology that puts private profits and jobs over human health and lives....All scientists having a personal stake in the development of commercial nuclear power should disqualify themselves from the nuclear power discussion and leave the field to citizens who are perfectly capable of determining what endangers them and their freedom.[5]

This quotation is revealing on a number of fronts. In the first place, the logic of the argument works against the speaker; for there is no reason to believe that Lorna Slazman (or any other member or official of groups like "Friends of the Earth") has any less of an interest in attacking nuclear power than nuclear scientists have in defending it. Following her own reasoning, officials like Salzman should disqualify themselves from the nuclear debate. Secondly, Salzman's statement implies that nuclear scientists are not citizens "capable of determining what endangers them and their freedom" and/or that the only "citizens" who will count in the debate and be allowed to be heard are those that are against nuclear power. Finally, it is evident from the foregoing quotation that "profit making" is as much the source of evil as the technology itself. Indeed, one *could* read the quotation in such a way that "commercial nuclear power" is to be objected to while government control is not. Such a reading, although probably somewhat inaccurate, indicates what is really at stake here—the control of industry by government with the government being run by the "right" groups.

If, for the sake of argument, we ignore the (primarily) ideological character of the anti-nuclear movement, we are left ostensibly with the moral question. Moral issues are decided presumably on criteria other than scientific evidence. That is why nuclear scientists are no more qualified to pass judgment on the nuclear power question than anyone else. But if we remove scientific evidence from the discussion of the nuclear issue in such areas as safety, health, and the environment, it is hard to know what is left that could be called a "moral issue." What seems to be left if scientific evidence is removed from moral discussion is (in the case of many anti-nuclear groups) a dislike of complicated technology and "profit making." At this point in our discussion, it should not be necessary to point out that such "dislikes" do not qualify as a basis for making categorical claims about social responsibility.

Of course, one may, now, wish to reintroduce scientific evidence into the moral debate on the grounds that it will show nuclear power to be unsafe and unhealthful as the church groups believe. A fair assessment of the issues in nuclear technology does not, however, lead to this unambiguous conclusion. Given that no technology is absolutely safe,[6] the safety and healthfullness of nuclear technology must be weighed against currently available alternative technologies. On this basis, nuclear power can look most attractive. Dr. Beckmann estimates, for example, that for every 1,000 MW of nuclear power that replaces coal power 20 to 100 lives are saved per year. At the time Dr. Beckmann made these estimates, nuclear power was saving 800 to 4,000 lives compared to coal. And roughly the same number of lives are in jeopardy for each year conversion to nuclear power is delayed.[7] Obviously, the production of coal will have to increase if we are to rely less and less on nuclear power. Beckmann goes even further and argues that nuclear power is superior to fossil fuels and coal in all areas: health, safety, the environment, waste disposal, risk, etc.[8] Beckmann makes *his* moral point as follows:

> Having flatly declared that the nuclear power issue cannot be left to scientists but must be settled by "citizen activity," they [Nader et. al.] cannot escape moral responsibility for these deaths. It would be callous enough to crusade against a technology that saves hundreds of lives every year, whatever the alleged motivation. But it is vile to crusade against it in the name of safety.[9]

My purpose, here, is not to use the same kind of tactics employed by the church groups. That is, I am not simply picking a scientist who agrees with my own ideology and then, in ignorance, making broad social claims about the obligations of others. My reasons for citing evidence contrary to popular myth are not to convince the reader of the benefits of nuclear technology nor to pretend that I am an expert on the issues. Rather, it is to say that the anti-nuclear forces have not presented an unqualified case requiring that utilities desist from nuclear power as a matter of social responsibility. Given the moral position outlined in the theoretical chapters, freedom can only be restricted if clear evidence of harm or the threat of harm has been established. To say this, however, is not necessarily to condone the current system of generating nuclear power. Since the utilities are not strictly liable for their behavior in this area, there could be less than adequate incentives to worry about safety. And since the government is responsible for most of the liability, we have another example of companies transferring their costs of doing business to the public. It must also be mentioned, though, that it is quite illogical to infer that since not everything is arranged properly, all activities in this area must be abandoned.

Because some questions of the safety of nuclear power still remain, I do not believe the Church groups necessarily have violated the first two principles in submitting their proxy resolutions. This is not to say that one should support their resolutions, but rather to say that the principle of moral consideration alone is operative here. If thoughtful reflection leads the stockholders to conclude that nuclear power plants should or should not be pursued, then the moral propriety of those judgments must be respected, even if one believes the basis upon which either side makes its judgment is faulty. The same type of comment would apply to any group submitting pro-nuclear proxy resolutions. The church groups do have one additional fact in their favor which they have not failed to exploit—namely, that it is now financially risky to invest in nuclear power. Consequently, some of the resolutions have a degree of responsibility about them that was missing in many of the other resolutions we examined.

As far as social responsibility goes, what I have said to this point is enough. Ambiguities about safety do present some opportunities for stockholder concern, even if not always in the form (or spirit) of the protesting church groups. But all things must be looked at in their broader context. The church proxy resolutions are part of a growing movement to put nuclear power, and utilities in general, under more government control and regulation. But even if one were to grant that there are safety problems related to nuclear power, it does not follow that more government control is the answer. Indeed, it may be *due* to government control that there are safety problems in the first place! I noted in the last chapter some of the general problems that crop up as a result of government regulation. Could it be that government interference has aggravated the problem, here, making the call for further control a call for further aggravation?[10] This could be the case if the incentives for safety are absent or actual disincentives have been created by government action, and there is some evidence to this effect.

Traditionally, incentives for safety and new ideas for the safe conduct of work in risky operations have come from a cooperative relationship between insurance companies and the business enterprises themselves. Safety inspectors were (and are) used to help set rates of firms in need of casualty insurance. If an inspector found safety problems, management had every incentive to comply with suggestions for improvement, for if they did not, their rates would increase. It was to the benefit of both parties to cooperate in safety improvements. This is still the way things are done in "harzardous" industries such as the chemical industry. In the early part of this century, however, legislation was passed by states (innocently enough) to require insurance companies to base their rates on actuarial experience. This legislation works only if there is acturial experience to be had, but if one is involved in a new industry, companies must look elsewhere or do without insurance. When nuclear power came into existence in the mid-fifties American companies were effectively prevented from insuring them. Overseas sources (for various reasons) could not meet the challange, so the industry turned to government for help. Instead of revising or overturning past law, the government's solution was to have a consortium of insurance companies provide limited coverage with the government itself being the "insurer of last resort." *The insurance industry has no role in checking on the safety of nuclear plants under this system.* This role has been filled by government agencies. As Dr. Adam Reed, an industrial consultant and faculty member of the New School for Social Research, notes:

> The Price-Anderson Act, which effected the government insurance scheme, had a very serious result. It cut all links between the nuclear power industry and new safety research findings developed in the laboratories of the insurance underwriters. The Nuclear Regulatory Commission, of course, imposed safety standards on the growing industry. But in 1979, its safety regulations were still based on the most recent safety research of *1954*.[11]

The cooperative relationship that provided incentives to safety in the past no longer exists. It is not simply that government mandated safety regulations are more often than not out of date (because there are no incentives for government agencies to be innovative and because changing a regulation once it is in force is extremely difficult) that is a cause for concern. More significant is the fact that the cooperative relationship that once existed has turned adversarial. As Dr. Reed puts it:

> Unlike the agent of a private insurance company, who can reward safety practices with lower premiums, a government inspector, who can only punish infractions, will command neither respect nor cooperation from a profit-oriented management. Indeed, his relationship to nuclear power plant managers is inherently adversary....A government inspector...outside a totalitarian society, cannot act on anything he cannot prove. And so instead of being corrected, safety problems are hidden....If an insurance company's safety consultant walked away from a policyholder's plant with a similar impression [that something was being hidden], the policyholder would soon be faced with a hefty increase in premiums. But the NRC, quite appropriately for a government agency, can do nothing without being able to prove specific violations.[12]

Comparisons with the chemical industry are not out of order, since many of the operations that take place in that industry are much more complicated than those that are a part of nuclear power generation. Dr. Reed continues his preceding point:

> Eli Lilly managers were doing their best to reduce insurance premiums by cooperating with safety consultants sent by their insurance company, while nuclear power company executives were doing *their* best to reduce the likelihood of fines by keeping AEC and NRC inspectors as much in the dark as possible; ...the workers at Eli

> Lilly were helped and encouraged to make their work stations safer, while the workers at nuclear power plants were forbidden to change anything without permission from Washington.[13]

If previous government interference and mismanagement could cause such problems, one wonders why so many critics advocate even *more* government control? It should certainly be evident that there are no moral obligations in this direction however much one is concerned about safety. On the other hand, one is again led to the suspicion that the church groups are more interested in having a cause than they are in unbiased concern for the safety of those they claim to represent.

### B. *The Production of Nuclear Arms*

In the case of companies manufacturing nuclear weapons or related products, the situation is rather different from the foregoing examples. The issue, here, is one of national defense and not one of corporate social responsibility. Given current U.S. arms policy, corporations are merely the means by which that policy is carried out. A company which manufactures nuclear weapons is not socially irresponsible in doing so. Indeed, a better case could be made that they are socially responsible, since they are carrying out the society's defense strategy. Therefore, if one has objections to current nuclear arms policy, the proper object of those protests should be the politicians who issue the defense contracts in the first place.

Two possible objections to this conclusion are likely. The first is that there is a higher law which no one, be they policy makers or mere implementers, can ignore. The supporting statement to the Union Carbide resolution puts it this way:

> At this critical point in time when the world daily confronts the prospect of Armaggedon, it is critical for individuals, corporations, and public servants to accept their roles as stewards of God's creation and to attempt to prevent such a development.[14]

It does seem that we are at a "critical" time with respect to nuclear arms. What is not clear is that a refusal by corporations to produce nuclear weapons will make this period any *less* critical. One would have to be prepared to say that the elimination of production by one side in the face of continued production by the other is morally obligatory, and this is far from obvious. Moreover, what the "higher law" specifies in this case is not as clear as, for example, what a "higher law" would have to say about an initiatory nuclear strike. The manufacturing of nuclear arms seems to be more a matter of ambiguity than of obligatory social responsibility.

The real problem does not seem to be a question of obedience to a higher law so much as it is a question of the extent to which corporations should be making foreign and defense policies. Despite our earlier criticisms of Theodore Levitt, this seems a good place to remember his worry about mixing corporations and public policy. If corporations were obligated to take an anti-nuclear arms position, they would be entering the realm of policy making. Unfortunately, our present mixed economy makes it quite difficult for corporations not to feel the pressure to get involved in public policy. The "Catch 22" is that if the no-mixing-in-public-policy principle is used to excuse corporations from having to take an anti-nuclear stand, it would also apply to any pressure corporations might exert to elect candidates with a more aggressive nuclear position. The only conclusion I can draw is that there ought to be a strong presumption against corporate involvement in public policy and a strong presumption in favor of the view that corporations producing goods for legitimate public projects cannot be said to be ignoring their social responsibilities.

The second objection to my view is related to what we have just said. It could be argued that corporations actually intensify the arms race by using their influence on Congressmen to secure an ever increasing source of lucrative government weapons contracts. Undoubtedly there exists lobbying of this type. Nevertheless, once this argument is made, it becomes evident that the same incentives and problems exist for any weapons system—not just nuclear weapons. As far as corporate social responsibility is concerned, the objection would have to be against any weapons production by corporations, which is absurd. My conclusion, then, would have to be along the lines of the one expressed in the last paragraph.

This chapter did not set out to exonerate industries connected with nuclear technology. But given the biased and selective (not to say ideological) nature of the way that this issue is currently discussed, an emphasis on some of the pro-nuclear arguments seemed necessary for the sake of balance. My conclusion must be that there is no obligation upon the nuclear industry in the name of social responsibility beyond what is stated by our three principles. Furthermore, there is no strong evidence that the industry is itself in violation of these principles or that the problems that do exist are not the result of the kinds of solutions advocated by industry critics.

# IX. Conclusion

If it were not for the presence of Chapter Three, I might have entitled this book "the myth of corporate social responsibility." In Chapter Two we saw the functionalists turn CSR into a myth by trying to remove the moral component from the concept of responsibility. Those who saw CSR as a moral question were to be replaced by "scientific," and thus morally neutral, accountants of the responsiveness of American business. On the other hand, those social permission theorists who clung to the idea that CSR was essentially a moral issue were shown to have defective theories. If Chapter Two is then coupled with Chapters Four through Eight which deal with practical matters, the idea of CSR seems to contain little credible content.

However, I also argued that the functionalists either need or smuggle in moral values, and that the social permission theorists were right about the moral character of the CSR debate. Nevertheless, the defects of the social permission theory did not disappear simply because they were correct about the moral nature of the debate. I, therefore, attempted in Chapter Three to present a theory based on moral values that would have both practical and theoretical appeal. That theory was grounded squarely on the sanctity of individual rights, but room was left for moral considerations that may arise even within the context of rights respecting actions. Using the theory discussed in Chapter Three, I then examined specific proposals on various topics in Chapters Four through Eight. These proposals grew out of a tacit or explicit acceptance of the social permission theory, and thus we saw how theoretical defects can lead to equally defective practical results and suggestions.

Although many arguments have been made in the foregoing pages, the *basic* point of this work has been to show that both the theoretical and practical advice given on corporate social responsibility is quite often not as compelling as first appearances might suggest. In making this point, I have argued that it is not morality per se that corporate critics represent. More often than not, such groups represent a moral or political position whose credentials are questionable. But the real problem is not simply an intellectual difference of opinion. In practice, the real problem comes down to the misuse of moral authority by those wielding power and respect in this area.

The church groups examined in the latter chapters are generally viewed as the guardians of our moral values. We have seen, however, that they have abused their position and have sometimes acted quite irresponsibly. Given the weight and sanctity of moral authority attached to these groups, the same concerns over abuses of power that they raise against corporations can be raised about their own behavior. In the long run, these groups will undermine their own cause; for instead of being seen as guardians of sound moral judgment, they will be looked upon as representatives of ideological enthusiasms.

> And when you fast, be not, as the hypocrites, sad; for they disfigure their faces, that to men they may appear fasting. Amen I say to you, they have received their reward.
>
> Matthew, VI, 16

# NOTES

*Chapter 1*

1. *Church Proxy Resolutions*, Interfaith Center on Corporate Responsibility, New York 1983.

2. *Ibid.,* p. i.

3. Joel. F. Henning, "Corporate Social Responsibility: Shell Game for the Seventies?" in *Corporate Power in America,* Ralph Nader and Mark J. Green (eds.) (New York: 1973), pp. 151-170.

4. Archie B. Carrol, *Business and Society: Managing Corporate Social Performance,* (Toronto: 1981), pp. 37-38.

5. Other texts offer similar accounts to the points I am making here (e.g., see Donald R. Harvey, *Business Policy and Strategic Management,* (Columbus, Ohio: 1982), Ch. 11; Keith Davis, William C. Frederick, Robert L. Blomstrom, *Business and Society:* Concepts and Policy Issues, (New York: 1980), Ch. 1.

6. *Ibid.,* pp. 48-51. A number of different authors are discussed in these pages.

7. Davis, Blomstrom, and Frederick, *op. cit.,* p. 5.

*Chapter 2*

1. John Ahrens and Fred D. Miller, Jr., "Corporate Democracy Act: Drastic and Mistaken Idea," *Toledo Blade* (April 13, 1980).

2. Howard F. Sohn, "The Social Responsibility Debate," *Journal of Business Ethics,* Vol. 1, No. 2, May 1982, pp. 139-144.

3. Sohn notes that there are others (e.g., John Corson and George Steiner) who would expand the scope of responsibility beyond what Friedman and Levitt would consider desirable. These thinkers are classified with Friedman and Levitt because the reason given for expanding CSR is to keep a positive business climate. Cf. *Ibid.,* p. 140.

4. Cf. Norman E. Bowie, "Changing the Rules" in *Ethical Theory and Business* (henceforth ETB), Tom L. Beauchamp and Norman E. Bowie (eds.), (Englewood Cliffs:

1983), pp. 103-106. Richard T. De George, *Business Ethics,* (New York: 1982), pp. 130-133. Thomas Donaldson, *Corporations and Morality,* (Englewood Cliffs: 1982), Ch. 3. Ralph Nader, "The Case for Federal Chartering," in *Corporate Power in America,* op. cit.

5. Robert Hessen, *In Defense of the Corporation,* (Stanford: 1982), pp. xiii-xiv and passim.

6. De George, *op. cit.,* pp. 103-106.

7. This group, perhaps best characterized by Keith Davis and Robert Blomstrom, would argue for conclusions quite different from Levitt's own.

8. Theodore Levitt, "The Dangers of Social Responsibility," in ETB, *op. cit.,* pp. 83-86. This article originally appeared in the *Harvard Business Review* in 1958.

9. Milton Friedman, "The Social Responsibility of Business," in ETB *op. cit.,* pp. 81-83. This piece is taken from Friedman's *Capitalism and Freedom,* and is reprinted or extensively summarized in almost every major text or book of readings on business ethics.

10. De George, *op. cit.,* pp. 103-106.

11. Friedman, *op. cit.,* p. 81.

12. What I have said could apply if business wins most of the battles as well. Levitt objects equally to the corporate state.

13. Laura L. Nash, "Ethics Without the Sermon," *Harvard Business Review,* Vol. 59, Nov.-Dec. 1981, p. 89. See my response in the letters to the editor section of the next issue of HBR.

14. Henry G. Manne, "Corporate Social Responsibility and Accountability," in *The Attack on Corporate America,* M. Bruce Johnson (ed.), (Coral Gables, Florida: 1978), p. 5.

15. The book, *The Attack on Corporate America, (op. cit.),* written primarily by economists, should demonstrate how dubious the social benefits will be if "socially responsible" recommendations are required. This book, however, pays little attention to moral theory. I mention it only to point out that the quasi-scientific pronouncements of "morally neutral" business texts on the benefits of CSR are seriously debatable.

16. Social permission theorists do not always equate "state" with "society." They do, however, believe that if the state is working properly regulatory policy should reflect the interests of society. This alteration will, in turn, allow for needed alterations of the rules for corporate behavior.

17. Any of the works of Ralph Nader will support this point. But most philosophers writing in the area would qualify as well. I examine some briefly below.

18. Robert Hessen, *In Defense of the Corporation, op. cit.*.

19. *Ibid.,* p. 26.

20. ETB, *op. cit.,* pp. 81-115.

21. Cf. Melvin Anshen, "Changing the Social Contract: A Role for Business," in *ibid.,* p. 97ff.

22. The Marxists seem more consistent here than those who wish to "have their capitalism and eat it too." For the Marxists would claim that business dictates all the terms, and hence there is no mutually agreeable arrangement either.

23. ETB, *op. cit.,* p. 103ff.

24. *Ibid.,* p. 105.

25. E.g., cf. Joel Feinberg, *Rights, Justice and the Bounds of Liberty,* (Princeton: 1980), Chs. 3-5. In the same text as the Bowie article (ETB, p. 89) John G. Simon, Charles W. Powers, and Jon P. Gunneman attempt to define "social injury." Their definition runs as follows: "...activities which violate, or frustrate the enforcement of, rules of domestic or international law intended to protect individuals against deprivation of health, safety or basic freedoms." The rather broad and ambiguous nature of this definition is more or less admitted by the authors. They hope, however, that "case law" will solve the ambiguity problems. But "case law" is informed (either explicitly or implicitly) by principles, and it is the question of principle that is at issue here (and to which this definition offers little help).

26. Cf. Fred D. Miller, Jr. "The Natural Right to Private Property," in *The Libertarian Reader,* (Totowa, New Jersey: 1982), pp. 275-285.

27. Keith Davis, "An Expanded View of the Social Responsibility of Business," in ETB, *op. cit.,* p. 95.

28. Thomas Donaldson, *op. cit.,* Ch. 3.

29. *Ibid.,* pp. 51-52.

30. *Ibid.,* p. 43. Condition 2 on this page of Donaldson's text seems to allow for the possibility of ownership of resources by business. However, since business is resourceless when it comes into the contract, and since "society" is treated as one party to the contract, the only reasonable conclusion to draw is that "society" will be dictating the terms.

31. *Ibid.,* p. 44.

32. *Ibid.,* p. 43.

33. *Ibid.,* p. 55.

34. Richard T. De George, "Can Corporations Have Moral Responsibility?" in ETB, *op. cit.,* pp. 66-67.

35. *Ibid.,* p. 66. Cf. also De George, Business Ethics, *op. cit.,* Ch. 8.

36. Cf. again *The Attack on Corporate America (op. cit.).* Some versions of welfare economics, however, might be used to support those moralists who seek a strong version of CSR.

### *Chapter 3*

1. Milton Friedman, *op. cit.,* p. 81.

2. While I believe my remarks will be true to Friedman's argument, I make no claim that my interpretation of his argument is necessarily the same as Friedman's own.

3. A common criticism is that American management is taught to take a short run "bottom line" approach. This is said to cause social problems which could be corrected if management took a longer run view. This may indeed be true, but it does not contribute much to the question here. For either management should take a long run view because it will make their firms more competitive (say with the Japanese), or it should take the long run because it is socially responsible even though it may diminish profitability or competitiveness. The first alternative is compatible with Friedman's argument, while the second alternative is not.

4. The individual human rights theory offered here should be regarded as only one possible variant of the individual agreement theory. There may also, for example, be a utilitarian or social contractarian version of the individual agreement theory.

5. John P. Kavanagh, "Ethical Issues in Plant Relocation," *Business and Professional Ethics Journal,* Winter 1982, p. 28. The phrase quoted here represents a part of Kavanagh's implied criticism of Friedman's argument.

6. E.g., cf. Robert Nozick, *Anarchy, State and Utopia,* (New York: 1974), pp. 28-35; Tibor Machan, *Human Rights and Human Liberties,* (Chicago: 1975); J. Charles King, "Moral Theory and the Foundations of Social Order," in *The Libertarian Reader, op. cit.,* pp. 16-36; Ellen Frankel Paul, "The Time-Frame Theory of Governmental Legitimacy," Eric Mack, "How to Derive Libertarian Rights," Douglas Den Uyl and Douglas Rasmussen, "Nozick on the Randian Argument," in *Reading Nozick,* Jeffrey Paul (ed.), (Totowa, New Jersey: 1981), pp. 270-285, 286-304, and 232-269 respectively.

7. Notice that I may legitimately frustrate your purposes without violating your rights as when I successfully get a job you and I were in competition for. But if I murder you or kidnap you to get that job, then I have prevented you from being able to formulate any plans or purposes of your own.

8. Retaliatory force (self-defense) would be legitimate as a response to initiatory force, but this is another issue.

9. It does not follow from this, however, that what one has a right to and what is right are completely separate issues. A number of the theories cited in 6 above make the connection at some point. What rights are supposed to do, however, is establish the conditions which must not be violated in human interaction. They are not designed to specify the complete moral life, which is why the term "side constraint" is appropriate here.

10. Cf. Gilbert Harmon, "Libertarianism and Morality," *The Libertarian Reader, op. cit.,* pp. 226ff.

11. It is worth noting here that many of those who wish to impose a strong positive version of CSR believe that it will benefit their cause to regard corporations as individuals. (e.g., cf. Donaldson as described above; but Donaldson also discusses some asymmetries in Ch. 2 and 6; James B. Wilber, "The Foundations of Corporate Responsibility," *Journal of Business Ethics,* Vol. 1, No. 2, May 1982; Peter French, "Corporate Moral Agency," in ETB, first edition, 1979; and Kenneth E. Goodpaster, "The Concept of Corporate Responsibility," in the *Journal of Business Ethics,* Vol. 2, No. 1, Feb. 1983. Most of these writers do note some disanalogies between corporations and individuals as well.) However, even if we were to regard corporations as individuals, the theory of rights proposed here would not generate more social responsibility than the state could require from individuals under this rights theory.

12. David, Frederick, and Blomstrom, *Business and Society, op. cit.,* p. 39.

13. To be accurate, Friedman's argument as I have presented it here is a moral argument. But that argument is abstracted out of many other things Friedman says about capitalism, productivity, and economic efficiency. Nevertheless, I do explain that part of Friedman's argument most often cited by others.

14. In fairness, it should be noted that the dichotomy expressed in the foregoing passage is likely to be accepted by some on the "right" as well as the "left." Thus many

free market economists are quite cynical about moral values and would concede to the other side the moral argument.

15. Quoted in *Business Week,* June 25, 1979.

16. *Ibid.*

17. Friedman, "The Social Responsibility of Business," *op. cit.,* p. 82.

18. As quoted in: Thomas M. Garrett, Raymond C. Baumhart, Theodore V. Purcell, Perry Roets, *Cases in Business Ethics,* (Englewood Cliffs: 1968), p. 293.

19. Friedman, however, is quite right to insist that this be determined by the market rather than by governmental dictate or tax incentives. My argument here rests on the supposition of a free market and not on mixed economy or welfare state foundations. Thus Friedman's ultimate rejection of the idea that the market should be subordinated for the sake of "social responsibility" is correct.

20. For a convenient summary, cf. Douglas Den Uyl and Tibor Machan, "Recent Work on the Concept of Happiness," *American Philosophical Quarterly,* Vol. 20, No. 2, April 1983, pp. 116-120.

21. "Happiness" (*eudaimonia*) often means something quite different for Aristotle than what the term may signify for a speaker of English. But we can safely ignore this issue, since our purpose here is merely to discuss the relationship among ends.

22. I thank a number of the managers present at the Liberty Fund, Inc. conference on business ethics (Fall 1981) for showing me this point. Most values pursued by managers (e.g., management techniques, financial accounting, investment strategies, etc.) are purely instrumental in character, although there may be moral dimensions to these values as well. Perhaps, then, what we have shown here is that moral values are never merely instrumental. It is also worth noting, however, that ("in the long run") corporations themselves are instrumental to the welfare of the individuals that own them. Corporations pursue profits to enhance the quality of life of their owners and not for the sake of the "social good." This point must be emphasized so that my remarks are not construed in social permission terms.

23. See Eirik Furbotn and Svetovar Pejovich, "Property Rights and Economic Theory: A Survey of Recent Literature," *Journal of Economic Literature,* Vol. X, No. 4, Dec. 1972, pp. 1148-1153.

*Chapter 4*

1. *Church Proxy Resolutions,* Interfaith Center on Corporate Responsibility, New York 1983.

2. *Ibid.,* p. i.

3. *Church Proxy Resolutions, op. cit.,* p. 58. Other companies to whom similar proposals were submitted include Perkin-Elmer (p. 62), Southern Company (p. 65), and Xerox (p. 72).

4. Since anti-market policies such as apartheid have economic costs, one would expect that economic forces would tend to force more toleration. There is evidence that this is happening in South Africa. If so, the impact would be more lasting than any policy of withdrawal or limitation.

5. Of course, if all the owners agree to the resolution, then managers would not be violating anyone's rights by following it. But the question here concerns the case of whether it would be right to enact the terms of the resolution in spite of what the rest of the owners want.

6. GM, Kodak, Johnson and Johnson, Control Data are mentioned in a supporting statement. p. 58.

7. *Church Proxy Resolutions, op. cit.,* p. 46.

8. *Ibid.*

9. *Ibid.*

10. This is not to deny that there may be situations where "improving the quality of employee's lives" may contribute to the welfare of the corporation. In that case, such actions would be legitimate; but it must be shown how these actions benefit the corporation in some way or do not hinder its goals.

11. It is worth noting again that there are no proxy resolutions in the Interfaith Center's publication which protest doing business with communist or socialist governments.

12. Cf. *Church Proxy Proposals, op. cit.,* pp. 50, 60, 66, and 70.

*Chapter 5*

1. *Church Proxy Resolutions, op. cit.,* p. 44.

2. *Ibid.,* p. 5.

3. *Ibid.,* pp. 3-4.

4. In the Allis-Chalmers resolution (*Ibid.* p. 2) we are told explicitly that "the church puts a premium on reinvestment in existing plants and communities."

5. Cf. Richard B. McKenzie, "Hostage Factories," *Reason Magazine,* April 1983, p. 39.

6. *Ibid.,* and see *Plant Closings: Public or Private Choices,* same author (editor), Cato Institute, (Washingtin D.C.,: 1982).

*Chapter 6*

1. *Cf. Church Proxy Resolutions, op. cit.,* pp. 6-10.

2. Carl Hoffman and John Reed, "When is Imbalance not Discrimination?" in *Discrimination, Affirmative Action, and Equal Opportunity,* W.E. Block and M.A. Walker (eds.), (The Fraser Institute: 1981) pp. 187-215.

3. The studies of Sowell and Williams can be found in *Ibid.,* Chs. 1 and 2.

4. *Ibid.,* Sowell, p. 59.

5. *Ibid.,* p. 53.

6. *Ibid.,* p. 10. I shall stick with the language of this resolution, but the more common reference is to the "comparable worth" concept.

7. John R. Schnembly, "Comparable Worth: A Legal Overview," *Personal Administrator* (Vol. 27, No. 4), pp. 43-48.

8. The continued fervor for comparable work is itself an example of the point I am making. Since coercively backed affirmative action programs and the like have not themselves closed the gap of aggregate income differentials and have created their own market distortions, more government intrusion (through comparable work) is being called for.

*Chapter 7*

1. *Church Proxy Resolutions, op. cit.,* pp. 27-28.

2. The text surrounding the actual resolution uses words, quite accurately, like "*suspected* human carcinogen" and "*potentially* dangerous levels." My purpose is not to mitigate the seriousness of the matter, but to indicate the difference between this language and the quotation below.

3. "The Clean Air Act," *The Heritage Foundation,* Aug. 2, 1982, p. 18.

4. Dwight R. Lee, "Environmental Versus Political Pollution," *International Institute for Economic Research,* Original Paper #39, Sept. 1982, p. 8.

5. E.g., cf. William Tucker, *Progress and Privilege: America in the Age of Environmentalism,* (Garden City: 1982.)

6. For a summary of how economists propose this might be done see A. Paul Baroutsis and Joseph Horton, "An Economic Strategy for Environmental Quality," Richard A. Gabriel and Sylvan Cohen (eds.), *The Environment: Critical Factors and Strategy Development* (New York: MSS Information Corporation, 1973).

7. John T. Dunlop, "The Limits of Legal Compulsion," in *A Managerial Odyssey*, Arthur Elkins and Dennis W. Callaghan (eds.), (Addison-Wesley Publishing Co., 1978) (second edition), pp. 368-375. Incredibly, Dunlop concludes that the solution to the problems given below is *different* government controls.

8. Peter H. Aranson, "Pollution Control: The Case for Competition," in *Instead of Regulation,* Robert Poole, Jr. (ed.), (Lexington, (Lexington, MA: 1982), pp. 368-381.

9. *Ibid.,* pp. 369-370.

10. *Ibid.,* p. 370.

11. *Ibid.,* p. 371.

12. For example, the professions represented by the members of the Sierra Club indicate that 3/4 of their members come from the upper classes of our society.

13. Aranson, p. 376.

14. *Ibid.,* p. 378.

15. *Ibid.,* p. 379.

16. *Ibid.,* pp. 380-381.

17. B. Peter Pashigian, "The Political Economy of the Clean Air Act: Regional Self-Interest in Environmental Legislation," *Center for the Study of American Business,* Formal Publication Number 51, Oct. 1982.

18. *Ibid.,* p. 4.

19. *Ibid.,* p. 10.

20. *Ibid.*

21. B. Peter Pashigian, "How Large and Small Plants Fare under Environmental Regulation," *Regulation,* Sept./Oct. 1983, pp. 19-23. The passage cited is taken from page 19.

22. *Ibid.,* p. 23.

23. Kenneth W. Chilton and Ronald J. Penoyer, "Making the Clean Air Act More Cost-Effective," *Center for the Study of American Business,* Formal Publication Number 42, Sept. 1981, pp. 11-17.

24. Neil Orloff, "Rethinking Environmental Law," *New York Times,* May 10, 1981, p. F3.

25. *Ibid.*

*Chapter 8*

1. *Church Proxy Resolutions, op. cit.,* pp. 13-24, and 75-87.

2. My own prejudice is that they are safer than these church groups claim. By the same token, I would be reluctant to *invest* in a utility heavily involved with nuclear power under current conditions.

3. *Church Proxy Resolutions,* p. 24.

4. The foregoing information comes from Petr Beckman, *The Health Hazards of Not Going Nuclear,* (New York: 1976), pp. 11-14.

5. *Ibid.,* pp. 15-16.

6. Incidentally, having no technology at all would be less safe and healthful than having technology.

7. Beckmann, p. 160.

8. See the various chapters of Beckmann's book.

9. *Ibid.,* p. 160.

10. I am ignoring here what may be the actual intentions of anti-nuclear groups—the complete removal of all nuclear power and technology. I am assuming, then, a serious concern for safety and truth.

11. Adam V. Reed, "Who Caused Three Mile Island?" *Reason Magazine,* August. 1980, pp. 16-23.

12. *Ibid.,* p. 22.

13. *Ibid.,* p. 23.

14. *Church Proxy Resolutions, op. cit.,* p. 83. Incidentally, this particular resolution is commending Union Carbide for withdrawing from weapons research and production.